Coming in to Land

Coming in to Land was premièred at the National Theatre, London in December 1986.

Stephen Poliakoff, born in 1952, was appointed Writer in Residence at the National Theatre for 1976 and the same year won the Evening Standard's Most Promising Playwright award for *Hitting Town* and *City Sugar*. His plays and films include *Clever Soldiers* (1974), *The Carnation Gang* (1974), *Heroes* (1975), *Strawberry Fields* (1977), *Stronger than the Sun* (1977), *Shout Across the River* (1978), *American Days* (1979), *The Summer Party* (1980), *Bloody Kids* (1980), *Caught on a Train* (1980), *Favourite Nights* (1981), *Soft Targets* (1982), *Runners* (1983), and *Breaking the Silence* (1984). He has also written and directed *Hidden City*, a film for Channel 4.

D0967706

STEPHEN POLIAKOFF

Coming in to Land

A METHUEN PAPERBACK

A METHUEN MODERN PLAY

First published in Great Britain as a Methuen Paperback original
in 1986 by Methuen London Ltd., 11 New Fetter Lane,
London EC4P 4EE and in the United States of America by
Methuen Inc., 29 West 35th Street, New York, NY 10001.

Set in IBM 10 point Journal by 🅰 Tek Art Ltd, Croydon, Surrey
Printed in Great Britain
by Richard Clay Ltd, Bungay, Suffolk

British Library Cataloguing in Publication Data

Poliakoff, Stephen
    Coming in to land. — (Methuen modern plays)
    I. Title
    822'. 914   PR6066.037

    ISBN 0-413-15430-0

Coming in to Land was first presented at the National Theatre, London on December 18, 1986 with the following cast:

HALINA	Maggie Smith
NEVILLE	Anthony Andrews
ANDREW	Andrew C. Wadsworth
PEIRCE	Tim Pigott-Smith
BOOTH	Michael Carter
WAVENEY	Ella Wilder
TURKISH WOMAN	Nezahat Hasan

Directed by Peter Hall
Designed by Alison Chitty
Lighting by Stephen Wentworth

PLACE: LONDON
TIME: NOW

ACT ONE

Scene One

Blue light, very early morning, the pastel-shaded walls of
NEVILLE's *flat.*
*The room is composed entirely of clean, soft, colours. There is
a large window, a plain expanse of glass, overlooking the
cyclorama.*
*There is hardly any furniture at all, bare walls with no marks
on them, and almost invisible cupboards, the doors and handles
of which blend imperceptibly into the pastel walls. There is a low
glass table, a black desk against the far wall with an electric
typewriter on it. The effect is of pale effortless spaciousness.*
*None of this is visible yet, there is dark blue light outside,
dawn coming up, an almost totally dark stage. The light continues
to change outside the window through the scene, sliding into a
crisp morning light.*
*News, jingles, and advertisements are coming out of a radio, in
the blue light, onto an empty stage. The news is about sterling
dropping, Russian arms control initiatives being greeted with
suspicion by the Foreign Office and local London traffic news,
all muddled in together.*
NEVILLE *comes onto the darkened stage, closely followed by*
ANDREW. NEVILLE *is in his mid thirties, and has an incisive
manner, authoritative and quick, but he also shows a sudden
charm. He is immaculately dressed in a grey suit.* ANDREW *is
the same age, ruffled worn appearance, an extraordinarily pale,
almost dead-white face.*

NEVILLE. I didn't realise you meant a *dawn* meeting. (*He
    smiles.*) I'm not really at my best this early.

ANDREW. Only time I could do it, I'm afraid.

The news continues in the background.

NEVILLE. It seems very appropriate somehow.

NEVILLE *moves around the stage switching on all the lights.*

Jesus it's cold! The heat wasn't even scheduled to come on. (*Glancing across at him.*) You look even paler than usual Andrew — it's all these odd hours you keep. Scurrying around London.

ANDREW (*switching off radio*). You are sure you're genuinely interested?

NEVILLE (*flicking on last light*). Interested in what?

ANDREW. In going through with this.

NEVILLE (*charming, authoritative*). Of course. I told you next time you needed someone I'd be willing (*Very slight pause.*) and I am. Now's the moment, it's easy for me.

ANDREW. She may not exactly be what you expected.

NEVILLE. This is the Polish woman — the one who came over with this Polish Student group?

ANDREW. Yes, 15 of them. *Mature* students on an exchange course, interior design at a College of Art.

NEVILLE (*smiles*). You haven't I hope brought 15 of them round now have you!

ANDREW (*seriously*). No, just the one. If you change your mind at this meeting and decide you can't do it, please let me know at *once,* that means during it, because everyday wasted makes it more difficult.

NEVILLE. I will. (*He smiles.*) I assure you.

HALINA *is standing in the doorway, behind them, half in darkness. She is wearing a very large bulky old grey coat, and carrying two huge plastic carrier bags which are stuffed to the brim, one of them is splashed with mud.*

She is in her late forties or early fifties, she stands in the doorway behind them, having put one bag down, puffing on a Polish cigarette, staring through a cloud of smoke.

NEVILLE. She does speak English?

HALINA (*from behind them*). Yes, I think so.

They turn and look at her.

Am I coming in too soon? Should I be outside still? (*She stands in doorway with bags.*) I was not completely sure what I was meant to do — whether I was waiting for a signal or not.

ANDREW. No, you can come in Halina.

HALINA (*moving with the large bags*). It is very good of you to make the time to see me, and maybe . . . (*Clouds of smoke pour round her.*) Excuse me, I have been smoking all night, waiting for this meeting.

ANDREW. This is Halina — Halina Sonya Rodziewizowna, that's right, isn't it?

HALINA. Yes (*To* NEVILLE:) how do you do?

NEVILLE (*shaking her hand*). Neville. (*Pronouncing her name differently:*) Shouldn't it be Rodiewizowna?

HALINA. Yes, I think so. That's even better.

HALINA *takes off her coat.*

It's very heavy I'm afraid (NEVILLE *takes it.*) the pockets are full of menus and theatre programmes, stuck together with chocolate — and peanut butter sandwiches (*Her voice trails off.*) there are all sorts of things in there.

She is wearing a strangely shaped grey dress underneath.

NEVILLE. I'm sorry about the temperature here — it won't be so freezing in a minute.

HALINA. It's not cold at all. (*Waving her arms.*) I'm very warm in fact.

NEVILLE *watches her with apprehension.*

ANDREW. Because of the strictly limited time for this meeting (*To* HALINA:) I always have to fit these in before my normal work, my conventional job, we must get down to the business at hand immediately.

Indicates HALINA *to sit on one of the very few chairs, she sits in her grey dress surrounded by her bags.*

HALINA. I must say before you begin, the absolutely, the completely last thing I want to do is cause anymore trouble.

ANDREW (*businesslike*). Of course. I usually ask at this stage (*Glancing at* NEVILLE.) when people aren't certain what to do (*Slight pause.*) is there any alternative?

HALINA *blows smoke, sitting in the centre of the stage.*

NEVILLE. Any other possible way of getting Halina in — other than marriage.

Pause.

(*Lightly looking across at* HALINA). Yes, it's essential to ask that I think.

ANDREW. LANDING Halina — to use the language of immigration officers. . . . we have to be brutally honest about the position.

HALINA (*staring about through smoke*). Please be brutal, yes.

ANDREW. It has to be a bald selection of pros and cons.

NEVILLE (*sitting at typewriter, deciding to take notes, beating out her name*). R-O-D-Z-I-E-W-I-Z-O-W-N-A.

He pronounces it perfectly.

HALINA (*startled*). That's right, yes.

ANDREW. Neville is infuriatingly good — at a surprising number of things. (*Moving across room, up and down, flicking out red and blue notebook.*) To start with the *cons* — with the negative factors.

Firstly, Halina has waited, which is usually fatal. There is a detestation of casual applications — unless you arrive screaming at the airport, I can't stand it back home and I'm not safe there, demanding immediate asylum, they are intensely suspicious, they are paranoid about all sorts of odds and sods being dumped on them from Eastern Europe.

HALINA (*blowing smoke*). I have waited far too long, yes.

NEVILLE (*typing*). Too late.

ANDREW. Secondly, every attempt to land is made in context — the context of world events, and that isn't too good at the moment is it. The recent sudden squall of East West tension, the expulsion of five Polish students in the US for industrial and military espionage, and three Russians from here.

HALINA. It is quite a bad time, yes.

NEVILLE (*types*). Wrong timing.

ANDREW. Moreover Halina does not wish to get involved in ritual 'hate' propaganda about her homeland, understandably.

(*Sharply.*) Lastly — Halina is not unfortunately a famous dissident, or even a member of Solidarity, no fashionable reason here, nor obviously is she something nationally desirable, like a ballerina, olympic athlete, boxer, squash player, or even a film director!

HALINA (*sitting with her bags, staring ahead*). No, I think that probably is right. (*Slight pause.*) I'm not.

NEVILLE (*typing*). Professional status — absent.

ANDREW. And that brings us to the personal history of the case, and the chances of media or parliamentary exploitation, of Halina.

NEVILLE. Which can be vital of course.

ANDREW. Is there any possible angle her story suggests?

NEVILLE (*lightly, looking across at* HALINA, *clasping her bags*). There must be something isn't there?

ANDREW (*briskly*). See if you can spot anything. As a child she is separated from her family for a few months during the war, and had to fend for herself on the streets of Warsaw, amongst the German troops. But that had a happy outcome, they are reunited, — nothing there. Next —

NEVILLE. Maybe Halina would like to tell us.

HALINA. Me? (*Pouring smoke.*) The big event, the one that is interesting, every *angle* leads back to my father. . . . and the large event is — he was found guilty of corruption, deceit, and incompetence. He was a member of the government, this is many years ago of course. He lived for ages afterwards, on and on, and on, I think you should tell it, it sounds much better when you do it.

ANDREW (*confident*). Her family plunged into semi-disgrace.

HALINA. Yes.

ANDREW. Her father, a minister, involved in the internecine party warfare of the Stalinist fifties, he loses, made to retire early from a government department to do with *Fish*. He isn't even thrown in prison!

NEVILLE. Really. He doesn't go to prison, at all?

ANDREW. No . . . His teenage daughter writes vigorous letters in his defence, he dies 29 years later having been cared for by said daughter, and drunk himself into oblivion.

NEVILLE. That *is* a long time.

ANDREW. Halina finds normal avenues to her all closed, she couldn't join the film school she very much wanted to, couldn't get into design college,

HALINA *staring ahead, blowing smoke.*

works occasionally as a part-time assistant for an elderly optician, and goes to design evening classes. *Finally* resulting in her being allowed to come over here on this course — reaching England.

Pause, HALINA *moves on chair holding one of her bags.*

But unfortunately this story is very mild, they've heard it a thousand times before.

HALINA. Yes, I know.

ANDREW. Even worse it's 32 years ago, there's no room now for subtle grey areas, mournful little tales from way back, only for something very strong, black and white.

ANDREW *moves.*

Halina is a victim of a tiny spec of history, no more than a pimple, so small the story wouldn't even show up on their screens, so to speak.

Pause.

She is too small to register.

Silence, HALINA *staring ahead.*

HALINA (*blowing smoke*). Absolutely.

NEVILLE (*watching* HALINA). And there is nothing else that is usable at all?

ANDREW. There is no real story, no.

NEVILLE (*laconic smile*). Maybe we ought to move on to the plus side now.

ANDREW. Of the plus side, the pluses — Halina is a woman. It is generally considered easier for women to land than men, because of the employment situation.

He stops, silence.

NEVILLE. That's it? That's all?

ANDREW. Yes — on a scale from A to G, I would put the chances of a straight application succeeding hovering between F and G.

Slight pause.

ANDREW. This analysis is devastating I know — and it is intended to be.

HALINA. Of course.

HALINA *moves with her heavy cluster of bags towards the window.*

NEVILLE. I think he maybe suggesting there is no alternative.

ANDREW. I am. (*He smiles.*) That is why she was put in touch with me.

NEVILLE (*watching her, sharp*). Halina — you can leave your bags, you don't have to take them everywhere with you.

HALINA. Yes.

HALINA *with her back to them by the window, sunlight and artificial light now mixing in the room.*

ANDREW (*pointedly*). Neville may need more time to decide if he's not too busy to do this.

NEVILLE. Yes. (*Staring at* HALINA.) I just have to weigh up a couple of things on my schedule.

HALINA (*by window*). You can see out now — what leafy, beautiful streets. (*Lightly.*) This is how I always imagined London to be, when I was small. Lush, tidy, squares just like this one. How marvellous to have such a view out of the window.

They both look at her.

ANDREW. Of course the secret of a successful landing with no media potential is picking the exact moment to move and where to do it.

NEVILLE. And how on earth do you decide that?

ANDREW. Everything has got more difficult — but there are still some very sleepy registrars left, who will merely mumble a few easy questions before they marry you.

HALINA. And you will find one of those?

ANDREW. Yes. (*To* NEVILLE.) As in every case a sudden international crisis can blow one out of the water on a single afternoon (*He moves.*) we're between crises at the moment, but if East West relations suddenly inflame further, a Warsaw Pact passport wanting to get married in the middle of that, they'll put it under the microscope. I often find myself racing against events, as they begin to brew, (*Sharp smile.*) so always listen to the news.

HALINA (*holding bags, facing them from the window*). There is a wonderful smell of coffee, I wonder where it's coming from?

NEVILLE (*not moving*). It's nearly ready, I'll get it in a minute.

ANDREW. I usually feel while things are at this stage — the PASSENGER, that's Halina naturally, is entitled to a word about the current marital status of the prospective 'husband'.

NEVILLE (*effortlessly*). Of course. Neville is single, and unlikely for recent personal reasons to wish to get genuinely married for the immediate future. (*Laconic smile.*) It suits me to be unavailable, for a certain time.

ANDREW. One of the reasons he's doing this I expect — thinking of helping us.

NEVILLE. Yes.

ANDREW (*telling* HALINA). And Neville is a reasonable and reliable person.

HALINA. Of course. (*Moving across the room with bags.*) I can tell that.

ANDREW. It is only fair to remind you this is an illegal act, there is a risk attached, it is very small, but it is there, and for Neville too, if he agrees to help us, as a member of the legal profession, he could face . . .

NEVILLE (*sharp*). We know this. (*Watching* HALINA.)

ANDREW. To lighten the atmosphere (*He smiles.*) this usually goes down well, I have a selection of rings here.

He pulls out a transparent plastic bag full of wedding rings.

Different sizes, they've all been used countless times of course, one or two are even gold, choose the one that fits and keep it.

HALINA (*spilling out rings to look at them*). What a lot of rings — you almost expect them all to have fingers still stuck in them.

NEVILLE (*watching* HALINA, *then pointing at rings*). I take it these were all *successes.*

ANDREW. Of course. If you decide to go ahead Neville, there is the question of accommodation — since landing Halina is going to be tough — a shared address for a few weeks *before* the marriage, in case of official investigation, even just for the post office would be desirable. It will cease immediately afterwards.

Bright early morning sunlight.

NEVILLE. Naturally, if I . . . Halina can stay here.

HALINA (*turning*). No, that will not be necessary, I'm causing too much bother already.

NEVILLE. It's no problem, there's a lot of space here.

HALINA *moving agitated with her bags.*

HALINA. Please — I don't want to be such a nuisance. I don't want to disrupt everything! Please do not let me, I needn't come here!

NEVILLE (*sharp*). It's *OK* — I told you.

Pause.

ANDREW (*steering him across room*). Neville — are you sure you want to do this, this is the time to say no.

NEVILLE. I realise that.

HALINA (*one of her bags has split open, pouring out its contents*). I'm sorry, I've already made a mess.

ANDREW (*with* NEVILLE). Obviously it will make a hell of a difference to Halina.

NEVILLE (*watching her*). I know. I don't need more time, I don't think (*Pause.*) I'm willing — I think. . . .

HALINA (*by window*). I do not want to look as if I'm begging.

Pause.

NEVILLE (*firm*). Yes . . . I've decided.

Pause.

I'll do it.

Blackout.
Burst of classical music.

Scene Two

PEIRCE's *office.*
    PEIRCE *and* BOOTH, *at a very small crowded desk, at the far side of the stage.*
    One of the pastel squares in the main wall has been removed, revealing a peeling flaking wall behind them, in the side wall there is a tiny yellow blind covering a window. There is just one chair, a very small desk, smothered in paper and files, and a clothes stand.

PEIRCE *is a short man in his forties. He is in shirtsleeves, just beginning to tie his tie. He is wearing running shoes.* BOOTH *is a tall dark-suited man, a little younger, with a large expressionless face.*

PEIRCE. Pass me my jacket and my tea in that order.

BOOTH *doesn't move.*

If you could be so kind. I don't mind drinking cold tea but I have to be properly dressed for them. Otherwise I don't function.

BOOTH *helps him on with his jacket.*

This is the worst part of the day — the beginning.

BOOTH *does not react.*

I expect you look forward to it.

BOOTH *passes tea.*

(*glancing through the yellow blind.*) My God, the queue grows larger every morning, it's seething around down there. (*He stands by the blind, noises coming from below.*) You know something interesting about this queue, it is not nearly as orderly and neatly shaped as when I first came here. They lined up as straight as an arrow then. (*Sipping tea by yellow blind.*) It looks an amazingly mixed bag today.

PEIRCE *turns.*

Right! Applications not processed from yesterday.

BOOTH, *totally expressionless, hands him large pile of files.* PEIRCE *glances in an instant at the name and date of each one.*

ABBAS — too late, by three days, no need to consider. Yilmaz too late, no need to consider. . . . Shanatram too late, Tomasial — owicz — too late (*Tossing files to the side.*) Smith, on time — but filled up the wrong form. (*Tosses it aside.*)

BOOTH *expressionless collects them, and puts them in out tray.*

The rest will have to wait — we'll do the same at lunchtime.

(PEIRCE *glances down at one of the files.*) It's amazing the number of different ways they find to spell LUNAR house, Lunar as in Looney, or Lunar as in Lewd.

PEIRCE *moves up to desk.*

I should have *three* sharpened AB pencils ready waiting here.

BOOTH *doesn't move.*

You couldn't be so kind.

BOOTH *starts sharpening pencils, a loud bell rings.*

Not yet! Can't let them in yet. I have not got my shoes on.

He starts changing his running shoes.

Once the door opens, this floor actually shakes, as they fight to get the best positions. Have you noticed that yet? The whole building seems to sway from side to side for just those first few moments as they stampede in.

BOOTH *deadpan sharpening pencils.*

Even the lavatories are full within the first few seconds, they'll flatten anything in their path, as they go up those stairs. (*Glancing at* BOOTH.) You will learn to avoid being out there for those opening minutes — it can be a very risky business. (*Doing up shoe-laces.*) God knows, their patience *after* that is incredible, phenomenal! They'll go without food for an entire day, and when you go out there, they stare at you with such longing.

Pause, noises from below.

Is there a clean handkerchief in that drawer?

BOOTH *doesn't move.*

If I could trouble you.

BOOTH *moves silently.*

I had an American girl in here yesterday, she *whispered* everything, this soft little voice. I couldn't hear her. Each time I leant forward to listen she got even quieter, fading a bit more with each question — until I was right up close to her mouth. Then suddenly she screams 'You bastard, just let me stay in this fucking country can't you!' Her saliva shot straight into me — a direct hit.

BOOTH *hands him a pristine white handkerchief.*

And two fake marriages last week. Haven't had one for a while, (*Sharp smile.*) maybe they're coming back into fashion. A particularly ludicrous couple, a young Chilean woman and this huge Glaswegian, covered in boils, they'd found for her from somewhere.

(PEIRCE *stands up sharply.*) I see you are your usual talkative self. I'm beginning to enjoy our little chats more and more.

Bells clamouring much louder.

Not yet!

He moves into position behind his desk. There is a loud clang, and a shadow of light across the back wall suggests the main doors opening.

Let us survive another day.

Blackout.

Scene Three

NEVILLE's *room: a few days later.*
   News items, as if radio channels are being changed: late-night music, and then domestic news settling on an item about whether the Russians are going to retaliate over the expulsion of three members of their embassy staff in London, so far threats have been issued, the report runs, but no action has been taken.
   The news mixes into the sound of torrential rain. Warm evening light in room. NEVILLE *and* HALINA *enter with gleaming umbrellas and wet coats, muddy water pouring out of* HALINA's *umbrella, she has also one of her large plastic bags with her which is very wet, its contents sodden at the top.*

NEVILLE. My God, what violent rain. (*He moves across the stage.*) It's probably the Fön.

HALINA. The What?

NEVILLE. The Fön (*Putting his umbrella sharply in the stand.*)

a warm wind they often get in Munich, it comes up from Africa, very occasionally it pierces as far are here, causing thunderstorms. (*He taps the thick glass of the window.*) It can't get in.

HALINA, *dropping her umbrella on chair, begins to unwind long sodden scarf.*

HALINA. I didn't realise you knew so much about the weather.

NEVILLE (*moving her umbrella and switching on his answering machine*). Did you enjoy the film?

HALINA (*unwinding her long scarf*). Yes — I liked it.

NEVILLE (*very surprised*). Really? The sort of film you feel evaporating before you're half way across the foyer.

A woman's voice comes out of the answering machine during NEVILLE's speech, 'where on earth have you been. . . . where've you been hiding yourself . . . are you free on Friday' etc.

(*charming but firm*). The attempt to make England a wild dark place was a little elephantine wasn't it, everybody popping up seething with trapped energy. (*He smiles.*) The English can't really make films. What about the play? this afternoon?

HALINA. Yes — I hated it.

NEVILLE (*sharp surprise*). Really? It did rather more than the usual boulevard comedy.

Another woman's voice curls out of the answering machine 'What have you been up to, . . . I thought you were going to call me . . . there's a party on Saturday, fancy dress, "fin de siècle", whatever that means'.

HALINA (*rolls up her scarf into big wet ball and sticks it unceremoniously into plastic bag*). Maybe there is a night film I could go and see. An *all* night showing, four movies together.

NEVILLE. Don't you think you've had enough Halina?

HALINA. Enough of what?

NEVILLE (*watching her*). Such an incessant diet of films and plays, you must have sampled nearly everything on offer, you're beginning to gorge yourself.

HALINA (*looks at him*). Certainly I'm gorging myself. (*Pause.*) You don't have to come with me to the things I . . .

NEVILLE (*cutting her off, very detached*). No, it helps, to make the story plausible, if anybody attempts to check before this marriage.

HALINA *takes off her heavy grey coat, she's wearing a new dress, in vivid, garishly-coloured squares. It doesn't fit her.*

HALINA. It's the only thing I've bought for myself yet, do you like the colour? It was a bargain of the week, tremendous value.

NEVILLE (*watching her, in the baggy dress*). So I can see.

HALINA. I like it.

NEVILLE (*very detached*). It's certainly a change of style, yes.

Old Woman's hoarse voice comes out of answering machine saying 'I still need to talk to you. I do . . . I do.' NEVILLE *switches it off.*

Not again! She's always on the tape, completely mad.

HALINA *is moving around, touching the sides, the walls, all the smooth unbroken surfaces, moving around his territory.*

HALINA. If you don't mind me saying so . . . everything is so clean here.

NEVILLE. Is it? (*Immediately picks up her wet coat.*) Nothing out of the ordinary.

HALINA (*beginning to touch every object in the room*). There's no trace of *anything.* There are no stains, no chipped paint, no spilt coffee, no dust even. You don't mind me touching, do you?

NEVILLE (*very warily, watching her*). No.

HALINA. And no sign of your work, if I had to say what does this person do?

NEVILLE (*sharp*). So you want to know more about my job? I told you I'm a solicitor.

HALINA. And?

NEVILLE (*sharp look*). It's a large firm, which has been moving more and more into the entertainment field, constant fights over client's copyright, their royalties, their inalienable rights, it's a real growth area. So much product is being spewed across the world, across frontiers, via satellites, there's all this money escaping into the ether, uncollected.

HALINA *moving through cupboard, finding the new invisible blending doors.*

HALINA. A successful young lawyer. And? . . . There's no sign of your friends, is Andrew a close friend?

NEVILLE (*warily*). Reasonably close. There were five of us, 'friends' at college in the late sixties, one's dead, one's in America, one writes successful books, and Andrew works for Shell and does his good works on the side, a peculiarly English arrangement, impossible to fully explain.

HALINA *looks at him.*

He started on Sunday afternoons, going to a charity in Peckham and helping out, and gradually he got involved in all of this. — And then there's me. (*Watching her closely.*) Who do you want to tell this to anyway?

HALINA (*ignoring him*). And?

Incessant sound of the torrential rain, HALINA *looking in every nook and cranny.*

NEVILLE. What do you mean, And?

HALINA. And there's no trace I can find of women. Girlfriends. Not even shoes in the cupboard, nothing squashed into the corners, not even anything in the bathroom.

NEVILLE. Really? You obviously haven't looked hard enough.

HALINA (*touching a chair*). No hair even. You must like them to totally remove themselves every night.

NEVILLE. Maybe. (*Laconic smile.*) I have just concluded a relationship in fact, rather messily, with a woman I've been seeing for several years. (*Sharp smile.*) One and a half

relationships to be more accurate. There was another girl,
a little younger. It was time for a change, all round.

HALINA. You prefer to be really independent obviously. (*At last
cupboard door.*) Who were those people gauling at us outside
the cinema?

NEVILLE. Gauping. I didn't see.

HALINA. I thought they were friends of yours, they were
pointing at you and me, you didn't seem to want to be
recognised with me, standing in the rain . . .

NEVILLE. I didn't notice, any of this.

HALINA. Gauping — I'm still collecting a few new words.
(*Sliding back cupboard door.*) It took me a long time to even
find the drinks here. (*Pouring herself a large whiskey.*) I can
have some more, can't I?

NEVILLE. If you want.

HALINA (*watching him*). Gauping — I started reading English
literature when I was very young, I learnt from all these large
ripe books, that's when I started thinking about England,
while I was nursing my Father. (*She throws back her head,
downs the whiskey, like vodka.*) I had the time.

NEVILLE. Yes, I wondered where you'd got your English from.

HALINA (*lightly, immediately pouring herself another glass*). I
was a young girl watching the manoeuvring and silent fighting
and party purges. These monstrous old men. I was near it all,
I even saw my father lose his job, through a half-opened door.
I was waiting in the passage for him, holding his galoshes. He
smashed two busts and two oil paintings and tried to set light
to his desk. He wouldn't let go of his official car for a whole
week, their cars meant a lot to them I assure you! He
personally drove it round and round Warsaw so nobody could
collect it. For the next thirty years he shouted at the wireless,
and then at the television, whenever any of his old colleagues
appeared, wallowing in rage and envy for being out man —

NEVILLE (*briskly, cutting her off*). Yes, you told us the story,
Halina I know that's why you're here. (*He moves to switch off*

a couple of lights.) By the way have any of the other Poles, Polish people, on your course, wondered about you moving in here?

HALINA. No.

NEVILLE *moves to exit,* HALINA *turns.*

Somebody rang up on the telephone about me, wanted to talk to me.

NEVILLE *stops.*

NEVILLE. Rang you here. Who?

HALINA. Somebody from a newspaper or maybe it was a television station.

NEVILLE. The way they smell out even the smallest fragment of a story! How on earth did they get onto you?

HALINA (*facing him*). They may have heard about the group of us at the college – in the present climate they were interested.

NEVILLE. What did they want from you?

HALINA. He yattered very fast – what did I think of England compared to Poland? I told him I didn't believe in facile comparisons, which I don't, that I'd resolved not to talk about this country till I knew it – and then he said is there anything else of interest about you?

NEVILLE (*watching her*). But he wasn't interested presumably because you had absolutely nothing to tell him.

Slight pause.

HALINA. That's correct.

NEVILLE. No small secrets swimming about anywhere Halina?

HALINA (*very slight pause*). No.

Sound of the torrential rain.

NEVILLE. Good. The arrangements are being made. You're safe here. (*He moves breezily.*) Turn out the lights please, and perhaps you could get rid of your plastic bags.

HALINA (*calls*). Neville!

NEVILLE *stops at exit.*

I can call you that — I am little unsure about using your first name.

NEVILLE. Of course. Since we are getting married, it seems appropriate.

HALINA. Neville seems the wrong name for you for some reason.

NEVILLE. Why? (*He begins to move again.*)

HALINA (*louder*). Neville. I have made a decision — I have to ask you something urgently.

He turns facing her, in her garish baggy dress.

Find me a job.

NEVILLE (*immediately*). It's out of the question, you haven't got a work permit.

HALINA. I *must* earn some money. I have lots of spare time on this course. I'll do anything for it, almost. I can do something for you?

NEVILLE. Like what?

HALINA. Cleaning is obviously not necessary (*Looking round.*) maybe a little typing, some sewing.

NEVILLE. Not required.

HALINA (*forcefully*). I'll do anything Neville — I can work in a shop, a back-street hotel, a Spaghetti Restaurant, you must have clients who — you must know somebody who'll need me.

NEVILLE. It's illegal Halina.

HALINA. People manage it all the time, you know they do.

NEVILLE. It's a totally unwarranted risk. Why . . .

HALINA. So many people have spent money on me over here, I must be able to pay it back, especially if something goes wrong.

NEVILLE. It can wait.

HALINA (*loud, facing him*). *Please* — I need to do this Neville.

NEVILLE (*very slight pause*). I'll sound out one of my clients, a Hi-Fi mogul, he owes me a favour, he's doing sensationally, always expanding, he may be able to fit you in sorting stock for Christmas somewhere.

HALINA. You will! You'll do it! (*Touching him.*) you don't know how pleased that makes me.

She kisses him, NEVILLE *flinches, embarrassed.*

Don't worry. I am not going to sample *everything* that's on offer around here.

Blackout.

Scene Four

The hi-fi and video emporium.
   News and music mixed together. The radio news concerning a clash between Russia and Britain over the expulsion of Soviet personnel from Britain, the Russians in retaliation have thrown out three Britons from Moscow; the channels change, end of an item about American statements on arms control. . . . the world news changes into a blast of local traffic news and then into the mild hum of Muzak.
   The hi-fi and video emporium suggested by three hi-fi towers about 8ft high, two of them crowned by televisions, sliding into place. They are spaced across the stage on the main pastel set. Two revolving stacks of cassettes are front stage, and a large blank video screen moves across the window upstage.
   Behind the screen the cyclorama gradually turning during scene from bright hard winter blue to a very sharp white.
   WAVENEY, *a black woman of 31, stands alone in the shop among the machines. She is beautifully dressed in very carefully chosen stylish clothes.*
   She is holding a very bulky glossy catalogue in front of her.

WAVENEY (*reading off catalogue*). The Pioneer 5770 EX, Price £780. Not in stock, unavailable at this store! (*Smile to herself.*) So don't ask for it. (*She moves among the machines.*)

The AIWA V1100 and V1200, price eleven hundred quid — never been in stock, never will be, unavailable at this store.

Looks through catalogue.

Jesus there are so many new machines in here; Loudspeakers —
the Wharfdale 708, price £450, haven't seen them round here,
not delivered to this shop, *never likely to be.*

She turns the page and smiles.

We must never forget the Panasonic NV870 — piles of them
for sale, they are dangling out of the window. Right!

*She puts down catalogue and picks up a pile of large
'REDUCED' labels.*

The Bargains start here! (*Standing over machine.*) Hitachi
MD50 — reduced from £699.99 pence to a wonderful seasonal
(*Slaps on label.*) £589.95.

Moving to another machine.

The AIWA 0800 with fully automatic DC Servo turntable and
linear tracking tone arm reduced to a sensational £749.99.
NO. (*Suddenly choosing another label.*) Why not an
unbelievable bargain of the year £599. (*Slaps the second label
on machine instead.*)

She moves.

The video screen — an ideal gift for the kids Christmas
stocking at a knockdown £1800 (*Slaps label on base of
screen. Then decides on second label.*) or why not an even
better £45.90! (*Slaps label on.*) Everything as far as you can
see reduced beyond your wildest dreams.

*She spins on her heel and slaps a £500 reduced sign on one of
the ordinary shop chairs and another on a stand up ashtray.*

HALINA *enters wearing a different stylish sweater over her
new dress, her grey coat hanging open.*

WAVENEY (*watching her approach*). You're late.

HALINA. I'm so very sorry. It's the first time I think.

WAVENEY. Maybe.

HALINA. It won't happen again.

WAVENEY. Maybe not.

HALINA (*looking about her at the machines*). What should I do? What needs doing first — is this the most important? (*Moving over to the revolving cassette stacks.*)

WAVENEY. *NO.* (*Mock anger.*) You haven't learnt all the stock yet — two weeks and you haven't mastered it! You must know the names of all the styluses.

HALINA. Styli.

WAVENEY. Styluses — what's this? (*She holds out a small plastic box.*)

HALINA *holds up box to light.*

HALINA. That's a Lingtons Sonatone STA.

WAVENEY. And this? (*Holding up another one.*)

HALINA. It's a stereo cartridge — a Nagouki.

WAVENEY. Wrong. A Nagoaka moving *permalloy* stereo cartridge MP30.

HALINA. Moving PERMALLOY. Nagoaka. I think that's fixed in my memory now, I hope. I'll take a few examples home, if I may, and study them — so I can get all their names.

WAVENEY. Yes, you'd better.

HALINA (*looking across the stage*). Does the Supervisor know I'm late?

WAVENEY. I have no idea where he is, probably staring longingly at some new stock somewhere, which he knows he'll never be able to order, never be able to touch! You should see how fantastically excited he gets by new equipment, new models. (*She waves the catalogue.*) The trade magazines are really erotic for him.

HALINA. That's how he gets his pleasure — I wondered why he was so pale.

WAVENEY. But I don't think he can keep this pretence up much longer. And we shouldn't either. It'll drive me crazy if we do.

HALINA. What pretence?

WAVENEY *standing among the gleaming machines.*

WAVENEY. What do you think? Where are the PEOPLE? Where

are they? (*She turns, loud.*) Didn't you wonder about it.

HALINA. A little.

WAVENEY. You thought this was how we did business in this country! — somehow people shuffle in here when we're not looking, buy things silently, leave their money in a collecting box, and vanish!

We have to admit it, somebody has finally got to say it. There are NO FUCKING CUSTOMERS. None.

She pushes one of the hi-fi towers, it rolls gently on its wheels across the stage. Pauses.

HALINA. I think I may have seen one yesterday.

WAVENEY. That was my daughter. The little girl that came in? That was my little eight-year-old daughter — she bought some record cleaners. Four weeks before Christmas I think we should be doing a little better than that.

HALINA. Maybe someone will come in *today*. You never know.

WAVENEY. You want a bet! (*She muses.*) It's been getting worse every month, creeping downward, first to a trickle, and then to a complete full stop. *Dead.* There are too many shops selling stuff like this.

HALINA. Yes. I'd noticed . . .

WAVENEY. Nine in this street alone. Soon be eating each other, you can already see the teeth marks on the door of this one. This was meant to be the start of a new chain too, of high-tech elegant shops, buy your video machines as if you're buying clothes at the most fashionable store, it obviously isn't catching on, is it! People just want to grab, buy it, and run . . .

HALINA. Why should they want to employ *me* here then?

WAVENEY. That's an interesting question. *Why*? Perhaps the owner of this joint didn't want to admit to your friend how badly things are going. (*She stops.*) I thought we'd got one for a moment — a customer.

HALINA (*watching*). Hovering . . . Gone! A near miss.

WAVENEY *leaning back against one of the hi-fi towers, pushing it gently across stage.*

WAVENEY. Haven't you got something you want to ask me, Halina?

HALINA (*innocently*). You mean where to find the audio-technica dual magnet phono cartridge?

WAVENEY. *NO.* (*She looks at* HALINA.) Don't you want to find out if I know what you did? You must want to tell someone about it, I think you may have to make do with me (*She smiles.*) you have to trust me . . .

Pause.

I saw what you did, Halina.

HALINA (*loud*). Really? (*She moves away apprehensively.*) When it happened?

WAVENEY. Yes. I turned round, suddenly there were thirteen of you — thirteen heads dotted all over the shop. (*Indicating televisions.*)

HALINA. Thirteen! (*She moves.*) They approached me, and then I was telling them, telling them my story. That's why I left early yesterday.

WAVENEY (*cutting her off*). How do you want to see it, big or small?

HALINA. See what?

WAVENEY. You — yourself of course. I recorded it, the early evening news, (*She moves among the machines.*) Let us use the wide-screen, why not? The bigger the better.

HALINA (*moving away*). I don't know if that's a very good idea Waveney, please don't.

WAVENEY. You have to see yourself — what is the point of having done it otherwise. You've got to use it, improve your technique.

HALINA (*moving to leave the room*). I think. . . . I must look at the catalogue now — I have to memorise the new range of Panasonic video recorders by the end of the day. . . .

WAVENEY (*as she starts V.H.S. machine*). I'll put it in black and white — because I prefer black and white.

HALINA *is right at the side of the stage when the enormous silent image of herself, her head in close up, appears on the video screen, mouth opening and closing, no volume as yet, clouds of smoke blowing out of her mouth, as on screen she tugs at a cigarette.* HALINA *stops at edge of stage, dwarfed by her own image, staring down at her, she turns away abruptly with her back to the screen.*

HALINA. I will not watch this.

The silent face moves for a moment on the screen, above them.

WAVENEY. Doesn't it look great! Now for your voice Halina.

She brings in the sound, booming sound, HALINA's *voice coming out of the screen, harshly and authoritatively.*

HALINA ON SCREEN (*sound comes in mid-sentence*). Yes, it was obviously a very frightening experience and without any warning, because one minute we were driving along, just an ordinary group of people, late one night after a party, in this old car, and the next we were bundled out, made to lie on the road, — and then what I can only call this nightmare began, without any reason, any cause.

HALINA *has turned during this to see herself speaking down from the screen, staring down from up there.*

HALINA. Oh my God! (*Looking up at herself.*) stop it, please stop the machine.

WAVENEY *freezes her image,* HALINA's *head caught staring ahead, her hat a little askew.*

What have I done — oh what have I done!

She waves her arms.

How could anybody believe a thing that looks like that — I look monstrous, like a creation from another planet.

WAVENEY (*smiles staring up*). The hat was a mistake I agree.

HALINA. Yes, I have never seen myself on television before — It seems to have photographed somebody else.

WAVENEY (*pointing at the frozen image of her with a broom*

handle like a lecturer). But the stare is good, fastening the audience with that gaze, trapping them in their seats, makes them think 'We have to listen to this woman' — it shows a natural instinct.

HALINA. I look like somebody who talks to themselves on trains.

WAVENEY (*sharp smile*). You look foreign, yes. A little odd — but that's no bad thing. If it happens again, the hands are far too busy, keep still, no twitching.

HALINA's *voice less loud as she moves again on screen.*

HALINA ON SCREEN. There were about five of them, police. 'You are under arrest,' they said. (*In reply to unseen questions:*) No, there was no charge made at all, they didn't even bother to look at our papers. Then they drove us at very high speed through the streets of Warsaw to the police station, and *that's* where everything happened . . .

HALINA (*facing her image on the screen as it talks*). I've done it now! I can't take it back. (*Points to herself.*) That weird looking object has gone out across the airwaves.

WAVENEY *suddenly stops the tape,* HALINA's *face caught staring down, her cigarette half raised,* NEVILLE *has entered.*

WAVENEY. A customer?

HALINA. No. I'm afraid not.

NEVILLE. There you are Halina. (*He looks up at the screen.*) And there.

HALINA. Yes, . . . (*Pause.*) I think I can explain.

NEVILLE *dwarfed by her massive image on screen, he looks from one to the other.*

NEVILLE. Clearly something has happened, how did you manage to get up there?

HALINA. There has been a little publicity about me.

NEVILLE (*staring at the huge head*). Little is not the word that immediately springs to mind.

WAVENEY (*watching him*). So *this* is your friend.

NEVILLE (*waving newspaper*). It's in here, too, the evening paper, your face staring out of page 5, above a story about an escaped python from Chessington zoo. (*He holds it up.*) Somebody catch you unawares did they — coax you into talking?

HALINA (*cutting him off*). No — I decided I had better tell my story.

NEVILLE. It's an extraordinary story Halina — we had no idea. You didn't tell me, you said there was nothing else.

HALINA. No I know, I thought I wasn't going to tell anyone. (*Looking at him.*) But I changed my mind.

NEVILLE (*reading off newspaper*). Polish housewife tells dramatic story, breaks ranks with visiting party. . . . her story throws disturbing light on what's still going on there, innocent citizens plucked out of their cars . . . arrested on New Year's Eve with friends . . . subjected to a startling and terrifying ordeal . . . prison guards . . .

HALINA (*staring at him*). Yes, the language is a little lurid in your newspapers, but that's what happened.

NEVILLE (*waving paper at screen*). This has implications Halina . . . have to calculate the life expectancy of the story, (*He smiles.*) we'll have some photographers at the wedding almost certainly, 'Solicitor marries Polish prison drama person' — a few lines —

HALINA. I have something to tell you which may have some relevance to the calculations.

Pause.

I don't want to marry you.

Pause.

NEVILLE (*slight smile, patient, slowly*). Halina — I am not sure you fully understand this is only an arrangement, to help you . . .

HALINA (*facing him across the breadth of the stage*). I know it's only an arrangement.

NEVILLE. This is a plan, a scheme to get you into the country, to land you, to outwit the immigration authorities.

HALINA. I don't think I can marry you — even as an arrangement.

Silence. HALINA's face staring down at him from the screen. NEVILLE stares from the screen to her.

NEVILLE (*sharp smile*). Is this some sort of Polish joke?

HALINA. No, no it's not.

NEVILLE (*moving up and down*). You must have moral scruples then? Are there religious reasons why . . .

HALINA. No, definitely not. I just don't want to marry you.

WAVENEY. That's clear enough isn't it.

HALINA (*staring at him*). Don't take it personally, please.

NEVILLE (*sharp smile*). I am not taking it personally I assure you, I'm merely curious.

HALINA's face moving on the screen without volume, WAVENEY has started the tape again, and is looking at HALINA onscreen, at her giant face, as NEVILLE talks.

(*His manner very effortless, sharp smile*). This must be one of the quickest rides from meeting — to engagement — to break up ever recorded. (*He glances between WAVENEY and HALINA.*) Has somebody else been advising you?

HALINA. No.

WAVENEY. Of course not.

NEVILLE (*appearing nonchalant*). It's alright, there's absolutely no need for me to know anymore, no explanation is necessary . . . (*Suddenly.*) has pressure been brought to bear on you?

HALINA. Absolutely not.

NEVILLE (*sharp*). Fine — I don't need to know. (*Staring at her.*) and — would you like to be found another candidate.

HALINA. As an arranged husband.

Momentary pause.

No, I don't think so.

NEVILLE. You don't sound absolutely sure.

HALINA. No (*Slight pause.*) I am. I've decided to get into this country by a different route, to tell my story.

NEVILLE (*swinging round sharp to* WAVENEY). Can you stop that machine please, I'm finding being dwarfed by her enormous head a little distracting.

WAVENEY (*suspicious, hostile*). You do, do you? I think she looks rather good up there, very powerful. I wouldn't mind having a spell up there myself. (*Defiant smile, to* HALINA.) I think I want to see you now in slow motion.

She puts the tape into slow motion, HALINA's *head moving on the screen, her mouth opening slowly, her head lifting up, the smoke coming out.*

NEVILLE (*cool smile*). This is what you get up to together here. How come you can splash yourself all over the equipment?

WAVENEY. Nobody minds.

NEVILLE. Why not.

WAVENEY. Because there are no customers as you can see.

NEVILLE. Don't be stupid — it's Christmas, the pre-Christmas boom time, locust time, people stripping whole shops bare.

HALINA. Where are they?

WAVENEY. Not here, they're not, nobody's stripping this place bare.

NEVILLE. A momentary lull, that's all, the stampede will start any moment.

WAVENEY. If *you* see a customer, it's such a rare sight — we may just photograph it and exhibit them in the window.

NEVILLE (*sharp*). I don't want to hear any more of that — this store is owned by a client and friend of mine. I would know if there were any difficulties.

WAVENEY (*loud*). I ought to know oughtn't I! I'm alone with
these machines — I lock them up at nights. (*She jangles a
bunch of keys.*) And dust them down in the morning. (*Defiant
smile.*) I'm the one that has to talk to them! (*She moves.*)
And I tell you this place is finished.

NEVILLE (*turning back to* HALINA). Maybe *you* could tell
yourself to stop moving up there.

HALINA*'s face moving very slowly above their heads.*

I don't know which Halina to talk to.

HALINA (*to* WAVENEY). *Yes.*

WAVENEY *stops the picture, freezes* HALINA *on the screen
staring ahead.*

NEVILLE (*sharp smile*). This is extraordinary Halina. You
peering down from that screen. (*He looks across at her.*) I
leave you unsupervised for 48 hours and you pop up all over
the media, handling it with alarming efficiency.

HALINA. Thank you.

NEVILLE (*detached smile*). You've only been in the country
a few weeks — and you've already had your 15 minutes of
fame.

HALINA (*immediately understanding the reference*). You mean
like the American painter Andy Warhol said, everyone famous
for 15 minutes. (*Slight smile.*) I hope to do better than that.

NEVILLE (*glancing at screen*). You want it to continue do you.

HALINA. Until I'm safely, completely inside this country, yes.

HALINA *moves, turns.*

I'll move out of course, you must want me to leave.

NEVILLE. Leave where?

HALINA. Your rooms — I'll put everything in a few bags
(*Indicates her plastic bag.*) I must be able to find a few more
of these, and move out tonight.

NEVILLE. Move out? Don't be stupid, why should I want you
to do that.

HALINA. You can't want me to stay, blocking up your apartment.

WAVENEY. If you're worried about where to go — I can find you a place.

NEVILLE. *NO* I don't want to hear anymore about that. (*Louder.*) That will not be necessary.

HALINA. If that's what you want.

NEVILLE (*sharp smile*). So that's why you were so desperate for me to find you a job? You thought you'd need the money when I threw you out on the street.

HALINA. Perhaps.

NEVILLE. I'm right. You planned that (*He smiles, moves up and down.*) You will have to be very careful from now on . . . each move you make will have to be considered, if you're going to get in because of what happened to you, applying in the normal way. (*He glances up at the screen.*) Because of the publicity you have to leave here at once of course. It's illegal for you to be here. (*Points to the image on screen.*) This must be erased at once, there must be no trace left here.

HALINA. Yes.

WAVENEY. *I'll* see to that — this is my equipment.

NEVILLE (*to* HALINA). And you'll need legal advice of course — timing of interviews, deadlines for application, somebody to check out the opposition, the immigration authorities.

HALINA (*interrupting*). I don't want a lawyer.

NEVILLE (*stops*). What on earth's got into you Halina . . . you need professional advice.

HALINA. I will *not* use a lawyer. I don't have to do I — I don't want to do it that way.

NEVILLE. But you need.

HALINA *is standing under her picture on the screen, two of them facing him.*

HALINA (*forceful*). I don't want a lawyer.

Pause.

NEVILLE. Right.

He moves.

Then I will have to act for you, unofficially, advise you. It's not my area of course, but I'll do it.

Pause. He looks at her.

That is − if it's acceptable to you Halina?

HALINA. If you want to do that. (*Slight pause.*) I'd be grateful.

HALINA's *face moving on screen again.*

NEVILLE (*smiles*). Thank God for that. One thing is settled. (*He moves towards* WAVENEY.) And now, if there's the possibility of any service round here.

WAVENEY. There might be . . .

NEVILLE. I think I'd better buy something (*Sharp disbelieving smile.*) − make sure this place lasts until Christmas at least!

Blackout.

Scene Five

PEIRCE's *office.*
The machines glide back off-stage, leaving for a moment HALINA's *picture on the screen lit by a spot, she is staring straight at us.*

Music, then a news item − HALINA's *story moving through the radio channels 'Polish housewife tells astonishing story . . . unprovoked ordeal . . . out of nowhere . . . out of the night of Warsaw . . . dramatic nightmare happenings in Polish police station . . . to ordinary citizens etc.*

NEVILLE *standing in* PEIRCE's *office. Another panel of the pastel-coloured walls comes away and stays away, making the office slightly bigger than before. The desk has also grown bigger, it is still covered in mounds of paper, and files, and a paper spike.*

Voices shouting in the distance, bells, a paper chain dangling incongruously on wall.

NEVILLE picks up metal spike on desk, PEIRCE enters rapidly, shouting as he comes.

PEIRCE. No, no more today. I can see no more. It is out of the question, I have finished.

Seeing NEVILLE, he stops.

PEIRCE. Been waiting long?

NEVILLE. No.

PEIRCE (*sounding disappointed.*) You haven't? (*Moves.*) You won't object then if I do certain things while we talk — it being Friday there are various urgent tasks to perform.

NEVILLE. Please feel free.

PEIRCE takes his sweater off with a sharp movement. On the hat stand there is a complete change of clothes.

PEIRCE. These off-the-cuff chats are becoming the fashion — people say they save time, I don't like them.

During following dialogue, he removes tie, changes shirt, slips track-suit bottom over his trousers, puts on casual shoes.

One doesn't want to take any of the place home with one, does one.

NEVILLE. I imagine not.

PEIRCE (*matter of fact*). One never knows what's been brought in here. (*As he begins to change.*) I have been interviewing all day, 15, maybe 18 different cases . . . a brother and sister from Ecuador looking enormously alike (*He looks up.*) suddenly I realised they were not brother and sister at all.

NEVILLE (*charming smile, one professional to another*). Obviously a full day . . . (*He picks up metal paper spike.*) I see you're allowed one of these.

PEIRCE. Allowed?

NEVILLE. Yes, when I was a solicitor in North London, a slightly decaying inner-city practice, *all* spikes were banned from all desks.

PEIRCE. What on earth for?

NEVILLE (*breezy smile*). Because as you sat there facing this succession of odd, often crazy clients, every now and then a particularly frustrated person would leap up and turn one of these (*He moves paper spike.*) into a deadly weapon — a lunge straight for the eye. (*Charming smile.*) I imagined it might be the same here.

PEIRCE (*sharp*). It is not. (*Finishing doing up a shoe.*) So what do you want to know?

NEVILLE. I have an acquaintance — a woman who I'm advising on a consultative, unofficial basis, I think you are aware of the case I am referring to.

PEIRCE. Yes.

NEVILLE. You are?

PEIRCE. I didn't say that.

NEVILLE. Halina Rodziewizowna, the Polish woman who was arrested on New Year's Eve in Warsaw. She's applied for residency — I wanted to know what you think her chances are?

PEIRCE (*looking up*). Her chances?

NEVILLE. Yes.

PEIRCE. Chances of success?

NEVILLE. Yes!

PEIRCE. You wouldn't want me to give you a straight answer about that.

NEVILLE. Wouldn't I?

PEIRCE. But unofficially, which is not necessarily worth having . . . I'd say have a go, should be, *almost* certainly, worth a try.

NEVILLE. You would advise that?

PEIRCE. I'm not advising anything.

NEVILLE. Of course not.

PEIRCE. Nor am I giving an opinion, I'm merely saying why not?

NEVILLE. Good. That seems clear.

PEIRCE (*beady, suspicious*). Does it? (*He moves.*) There are minus points of course — no request for asylum, application delayed until it's far too late, a Polish passport — always a major liability, near Christmas, the worst time possible, delays often prolonged, could easily prevent even a short extension to her visa.

NEVILLE. On a scale from one to ten, where would you . . .

PEIRCE. No! Not the scale of one to ten please — that always comes up, I never respond to it.

NEVILLE. Below five?

PEIRCE. Below six.

Pause.

NEVILLE. I see.

PEIRCE (*surprised, sharp*). Do you? (*Stands by yellowing blind, glancing out.*) The patterns people make in the snow, extra-ordinary neurotic shapes as they have a last cigarette before they drag themselves away from the building. You're suddenly able to see all sorts of things in this weather. . . . that weren't visible before.

NEVILLE (*puzzled by this, breezy smile*). The snow won't last — it never does.

PEIRCE (*beady, turning*). Of course it depends slightly on who she comes up in front of — your acquaintance — which officer does the interviewing.

NEVILLE. Naturally. Have you any idea who that might be?

PEIRCE. Some officers are more taxing than others — *I* can usually tell in ten minutes, the average hovers between 10 and 15 minutes; it's normally blindingly obvious if there are any discrepancies in what they say, in the passenger's version.

NEVILLE. So she'll be seeing you will she?

PEIRCE. I don't think you'd want me to answer that question.

NEVILLE (*slight smile*). No . . . of course not.

> PERICE *takes a handful of papers, with brisk movements he tears them up.*

PEIRCE. PUBLICITY — is another matter isn't it? If there has been some, and I'm not saying if I'm aware of any or not, generally we take a very dim view of people that have gone public before coming to us.

NEVILLE. I'll make absolutely sure there's no more of that — it will be stopped as from now. If you'd like I'll fill you . . .

PEIRCE (*holding up his hand*). No, no, save it, no facts please — we want it fresh. Absolutely fresh.

> PEIRCE *stares down at the tape recorder on desk.*

I have one small task to perform before I go. (*Looks up.*) to rewind the tape and see what we've netted during last night.

NEVILLE. What's been netted?

PEIRCE. Yes, information that has come in . . . People informing about cases under consideration.

> PEIRCE *zips up track suit with a sudden single movement.*

NEVILLE (*surprised*). Informing? Really? (*Then more urbane.*) I knew some of this must go on of course — but I've never seen the results before.

> *Both staring down into the tape.*

PEIRCE. Yes, it's a consistent source of intelligence, a constant and valuable flow.

> PEIRCE *switching the tape volume up, we hear the loud blank hiss of the empty tape, interrupted several times by a click of people ringing in but not leaving a message.* NEVILLE *moves, assuming he has to leave.*

No Mr Gregory, you don't have to go yet. If there's anything on here, I will stop it when we reach it.

NEVILLE (*surprised but pleased, moving back to the tape*). So you get all these informers on tape, it must make interesting listening.

PEIRCE. Yes, it's a 24-hour service — when there isn't a duty office available, we resort to just the machine.

Loud click on the machine, noise of somebody breathing into the receiver nervously, then ringing off. PEIRCE *looks down.*

People get to the water, but they don't always drink. Their nerve fails and they slip away. It's a very poor catch today, I'm afraid. On a good night sometimes the tape is jam packed from end to end, with a whole cross-section of nationalities.

There's a wild soft jabber suddenly on the tape in a difficult to recognise language, and then the speaker disappears.

NEVILLE. I think that was probably Persian. Yes, Iranian Arabic.

PEIRCE. Really? Is that what it was. He slid off the hook anyway. (*Glancing at tape.*) They often tend to come in a rush, squashed together on the same part of the tape, about 2.am at night, that's their favourite time — suddenly there they are.

NEVILLE (*moving close, fascinated*). All moved to call at the same witching hour. (*He looks at* PEIRCE.) Why do they do it, inform? It can't be greed, you don't pay them?

PEIRCE. Absolutely not. They do it to get rid of 'friends' and relatives; they don't like — or detest. Or because they're not doing as well over here as they hoped and are very resentful.

PEIRCE *turning to look at him.*

It's safe to say their motives vary.

NEVILLE (*intrigued smile, staring down at machine*). There're a lot of curious people out there, swimming about at 2 o'clock in the morning.

Suddenly a voice, urgent, stabbing out of the tape. 'Are you there, are you listening I want to tell you about, I have to tell you everything I know about Marie, about how she's really not, not, NOT . . .' PEIRCE *clicks off tape before it goes further.*

PEIRCE. Some people shout, I'm afraid . . . You must leave me to my listening now.

NEVILLE *moves.*

You wouldn't want me to wish you good luck — so I'm not going to.

Blackout.

Scene Six

NEVILLE'*s flat.*

   The last seconds of a radio commercial, followed by a mention of HALINA'*s experience on a late-night radio phone-in, which blends into the sound of carols being sung outside the window, in the square, in the distance at first.*

   Snow pouring down the cyclorama, heavy incessant snow, for a moment back-lit, forming a white Dickensian Christmas scene outside.

   Inside, a small Christmas tree stands at the far end of the room with coloured lights and decorations on it, among the clean pastel walls. The lights in room come up only half way leaving a late-night feel.

   As the angelic sound of the high voices singing the carol, 'Good King Wenceslas', get nearer and pass right below the window we hear the lyrics to the familiar tune are darker, obscene, unsettling, still sung by the high voices. A hooligan version. The voices take some time to recede during the following dialogue.

   ANDREW *standing with his back to the audience watching the snow drive down.* HALINA *in her long heavy coat,* NEVILLE *is opening a bottle of champagne.*

ANDREW. My God has it ever snowed like this. This is *London* doesn't it realise that! It's far too deep, it's lying there like it's never going to leave.

Carol singers approaching.

NEVILLE (*opening champagne*). I see no reason why we shouldn't have the champagne — even though there is nothing to celebrate. No date for Halina's interview.

HALINA. Yet. (*She takes her glass of champagne, moves round the room by herself.*)

NEVILLE. What an extraordinary noise!

Carol singers right underneath.

It's nearly 3 o'clock in the morning, what are they doing.

ANDREW. Yes. X certificate carol singers moving down below. They look a fairly grisly terrifying collection to me.

NEVILLE. I've never heard that sound in the square before.

ANDREW. Maybe they only come out when we have a really bad winter.

ANDREW *takes his champagne from* NEVILLE, *boyish manner together.*

I see you still haven't read the book — Christopher's new book I lent you.

NEVILLE (*clicking on his answering machine*). I read half a page.

ANDREW (*sharp smile*). As much as that!

NEVILLE (*picking up book*). It was precisely how I'd imagined it'd be, very bland — and extremely short.

ANDREW. You pick it up like it's going to scald you! (*He smiles.*) I think you may be a little jealous.

Soft woman's voice leaking out of the answering machine.

NEVILLE (*charming smile*). Jealous? Slightly, I admit. It's not exactly gnawing inside though, more a very mild hum. It occasionally spurts out when I catch sight of him in one of the Sunday papers.

Voice urgent, stabbing out of the answering machine, the hoarse OLD WOMAN's *voice we heard in Scene Three, asking when she can see* NEVILLE.

OLD WOMAN'S VOICE. I have to see you about my house, they're trying to get me out of my house. I have to stay in all day, I know they are coming . . .

NEVILLE (*clicking machine off*). Just one of my old ex-clients — she still pursues me, obsessed with a problem she'll never let go of, about her house! (*Looking at machine.*) No news for Halina though.

HALINA *moves offstage in her long coat, carol singers in distance.*

(*Watching her, as soon as she's left*). It's been a peculiar few weeks, I can tell you. She's a slightly batty character of course . . .

ANDREW. Is she?

NEVILLE. Oh yes — but curiously interesting. I like the thought of her being a witness to these bits of recent history, rather vivid slices, the German occupation, the Stalinist struggles —

ANDREW (*smile*). And having all that right here in your room.

NEVILLE. But what's really intriguing about Halina is . . . (*He smiles.*) she's a long way from being a wholly admirable person.

ANDREW (*indicating flat*). She's probably a little shy — a little nervous of all this.

NEVILLE (*suddenly*). They have to at least *see* her here don't they, give her an interview.

ANDREW. I'd say yes, normally they would.

NEVILLE (*cutting him off*). The immigration officer I saw was a real shifty little creep, just like one'ed imagine them to be — he even seemed to be showing off his intelligence operation to me.

HALINA *enters behind them. They don't notice.*

ANDREW. They will delay as long as they can of course.

NEVILLE. And then say it's too late.

ANDREW. It's possible they may never see her, but of course the publicity is good, and what happened to her in Poland is very strong . . .

HALINA *topples sideways, brushing the side wall, she breaks her fall, steadying herself.*

NEVILLE. Halina?

ANDREW. Are you all right?

HALINA (*calmly refilling her glass*). I'm very well. (*Her manner and voice are not drunk at all.*)

NEVILLE (*watching her with glass*). She must eat something. She hardly ate anything in the restaurant did you Halina?

HALINA. No, but I can assure you I didn't waste it, when you weren't looking, old habits die very slowly, I managed to bring it back home.

HALINA is kneeling unselfconsciously in her heavy coat in the middle of the stage, she reaches into the pockets.

NEVILLE. No wonder you were walking so far behind.

HALINA. These deep pockets are very useful, this is a coat for gourmets. (*Slight smile.*) Now I've been deprived of my bags, it has become even more valuable. There're a lot of recent meals down there, the sauces running together (*Indicates left pocket.*) fish and seafood are on this side . . .

HALINA bends her head, kneeling in middle of room, eating small piece of bread from her pocket. NEVILLE watching her.

NEVILLE. Halina.

She looks up.

It's not true, is it?

HALINA. What's not true?

NEVILLE. Your story, the armed guards, the prison yard, the whole dramatic ordeal — you made it all up.

HALINA (*giving nothing away*). What makes you say that?

ANDREW (*louder*). Is your story *true* Halina?

Slight pause.

HALINA. Not exactly.

NEVILLE. Not exactly? (*Sharp.*) Is it true or not?

HALINA. We were arrested on New Year's Eve . . .

NEVILLE. You *were.*

HALINA. A group of us were driving in a car which wasn't properly licensed, there was a little confusion about our papers as well, they were being lazy, the police because it was a holiday, so we were held for about 48 hours in the station playing cards and drinking a little and smoking a lot. Then they let us go.

NEVILLE. That's all! No drama, no nightmare?

HALINA. That is everything — That's what happened.

Snow outside.

ANDREW. Jesus! I believed it. I believed her story.

NEVILLE (*very quick*). *That's* why you didn't want a lawyer, because it isn't true!

HALINA (*correcting him*). I had to improve on the truth, a little. It was obvious from everything you said I needed something stronger, darker. (*Lightly.*) Something more than just being the victim of a tiny pimple of history. So I did.

Carol singers beginning to cross square again in distance.

ANDREW. My God! (*Moving rapidly.*) I have to make some quick calculations — the risk factor?

NEVILLE. Which is what?

ANDREW. Of course people trying to land often lie, sometimes very elaborately and on rare occasions a few get in that way.

NEVILLE (*sharp, sceptical*). Really? People do?

ANDREW. I personally know of at least two cases. It's incredibly difficult not to get tripped in the interrogation — but it can be done.

NEVILLE. But will they believe she was allowed out of Poland, if this is *meant* to have happened?

ANDREW (*precise*). That's not a problem. Either the Polish authorities didn't know — Halina too frightened to tell etc., or they let her go because they wanted to get rid of her, dump her out of the country.

Halina can choose which she goes with — the British will buy either — *IF* they believe her story.

NEVILLE. And will they?

ANDREW (*pacing, calculating*). She *was* in prison, they can check that if they like. They will never be able to confirm or deny what went on there. The Poles will say it's all lies, the British won't believe a single bloody thing they say — now it's a tremendous advantage it's Christmas time, everything moving so sluggishly here, they may not look too hard. It will all depend on the interview, it's a strong story, they may like its melodrama, it's what they expect . . .

NEVILLE. What are the chances, Andrew?

ANDREW (*stops pacing*). If you want a first estimate . . . and this is very much a first estimate . . . 75/25.

HALINA. In my favour?

ANDREW. No, in their favour of course.

HALINA *turns.*

The odds always favour them.

NEVILLE. She hasn't a hope, I've seen the opposition. She hasn't a chance!

ANDREW. Of course there is still the possibility if she failed, even if they were told her story was false and proved it, of reverting to the original plan.

NEVILLE. There is? Going ahead with the original scheme?

ANDREW. Yes, obviously the longer we delay on that, the more difficult it becomes.

NEVILLE. Obviously.

ANDREW. It would need to be exceptionally convincing. (*Pacing.*) I should say the same odds apply. Of course, if outside events suddenly change, a quick extra freeze of East West relations, if it suits them to let . . .

NEVILLE (*staring at* HALINA). I think you better leave us Andrew.

HALINA (*sharp*). Why?

ANDREW (*suddenly stops pacing*). Yes, I have an appointment.

HALINA. What? At 3.30 in the morning?

ANDREW (*moving to exit*). Yes, it never seems to stop, I have to fit some of my cases in at strange hours. People hanging on by their finger tips, about to be thrown out of the country — and getting around in this snow takes twice as long as usual. I'll be in touch.

He's gone.

Pause, NEVILLE *looking across at* HALINA.

NEVILLE (*very icy*). So Halina — what are you *really* up to?

HALINA. Just what you see.

NEVILLE. What sort of answer is that?

The snow increasing all the time.

HALINA. It's the only one I can give you.

NEVILLE (*moving towards her, sharp, legal*). But that is simply not the case is it. Why all these lies?

HALINA. What lies?

NEVILLE. Come on Halina, the psychotic guards, the prison drama, you've taken a ridiculous risk.

HALINA. I do not agree.

NEVILLE. They'll crack your story in a few minutes. (*Sharp smile.*) Between 10 and 15 minutes to be precise. We had a perfectly simple arrangement.

HALINA *facing him, very still.*

HALINA. I know. It was a choice between the devil and the deep black sea.

NEVILLE. Is that deliberate?

HALINA *doesn't move.*

(*Crisp.*) Halina, I am a rational man — and I want some reasons now.

HALINA (*surprised*). For what?

NEVILLE (*louder*). What are you trying to do?

HALINA *moving, taking her heavy coat off, underneath the fashionable sweater and a new skirt.*

HALINA. I am just trying to get into the country — your country.

NEVILLE. I don't believe that's all that's going on, why did you come over to England *NOW*, at this precise moment.

HALINA (*facing him*). I've told you, why can't you accept it. I was taking care of my Father, I had years of sitting at the end of his bed, his voice still goes round and round my head every night. And then he died.

I had to make up for lost time. And I couldn't do it in Poland.

Snowing increasing outside. Carol singers in distance.

NEVILLE (*moving up to her*). From what I've seen of you Halina, I can believe in you as a little girl scuttling around Warsaw by yourself, dodging between the German tanks, but I don't believe for one moment, in you sitting quietly at your father's bedside for the rest of your life.

HALINA. It doesn't make any difference what you believe. That's what I had to do (*Lightly.*) I'm not expecting you to shed tears over it.

NEVILLE. Who sent you here?

HALINA. What do you mean who sent me? That's so predictable Neville, you must stop thinking that I have some spy contact, feeding squirrels in the park by the litter bins, forever waiting for me to show up.

NEVILLE (*watching*). Are you a communist Halina?

HALINA. That's not really your business is it? I lost all my politics in my twenties, while I was on this island, so to speak, with my father. (*Facing him.*) I'm only just re-emerging to look around.

NEVILLE (*bearing down on her*). Really? So how on earth did you know enough to use the media the way you did? Pitch your story so right?

HALINA (*slight smile*). Oh that's simple, that's easy, all the repeat programmes on the BBC we have, like the Forsyte Saga.

Pause.

NEVILLE. Why don't you surprise me Halina? Give me a straight answer for once.

HALINA. That was. I think I watched every English television programme ever shown in Poland. I'm full of English trivia.

NEVILLE (*sharp*). I thought you were meant to be a harmless Polish 'housewife' interested in wallpaper design! Who didn't want to get involved in East West propaganda (*Flaps newspaper.*) And now look what you've achieved with your story.

HALINA (*cutting him off*). I didn't want to get involved in painting an even worse picture of the East than already exists, going before some tiny official and debasing myself with cold-war platitudes, but the police are different — a story about them. They can look after themselves.

NEVILLE. The distinction seems far from obvious to me.

HALINA (*facing him*). It's the price of admission — isn't that right? (*Pause.*) Of getting in here.

Silence. Snow even harder.

NEVILLE (*suspicious*). You keep changing Halina.

HALINA. Do I?

NEVILLE. Yes, one moment you're this comic character emerging with a heap of scabby plastic bags that you won't let out of your sight. And now you look like this. You seem to have gone through the voracious buying — the first — thing — you — see stage to something else amazingly quickly.

HALINA (*watching him*). You mean from bad taste to style in two easy leaps. (*Indicating clothes.*) I just borrowed these.

NEVILLE (*pointing out*). And outside here — outside this window, odd things keep happening. There's this violent vivid un-English weather.

HALINA. So I am to blame for the weather as well!

NEVILLE. And then across this snow-covered scene these weird psychopathic carol singers wander singing sweet murderous songs — unlike anything I've ever heard before! I come into a friend's video shop and you immediately claim it is about to go bust. . . . which is rubbish of course.

HALINA. Why should I make something like that up!

NEVILLE. I feel I'm inhabiting one of those infuriating East European cartoons they show before the main feature in art houses where everything keeps changing shape, while a little blob like man travels through it all making squeaking noises!

HALINA (*watching him*). Yes.

Pause.

Your room's a little different too, Neville.

NEVILLE (*looking around*). What do you mean?

HALINA. It's been searched.

NEVILLE. Searched? Rubbish.

HALINA *indicates low soft white chair.*

HALINA. This chair has been moved several inches from where it was before.

NEVILLE. I see no difference.

HALINA. He's left a rather more obvious sign I'm afraid, I have a nose for these things.

She lifts cushions on chair. The inside of pale white armchair is smeared with oil stains, heavy black stains.

NEVILLE (*suspicious*). What's that?

HALINA. He seems to have been bleeding oil (*She smiles.*) his motorcycle must have been leaking and he brought a lot in with him.

She moves one of the few decorations on the wall, underneath it black oil fingermarks smeared.

Probably a little bit of it under most things, smeared his little fingers everywhere. Rather an amateur effort by our standards back home.

NEVILLE (*sharp*). They've been inside here! In my flat — what on earth for?

HALINA. They decided to run a check on me (*Looks up.*) maybe they think like you.

NEVILLE. My God. Halina (*He moves.*) it is clear what should happen now. It would be so simple — you ought to revert to the original plan. You can marry me.

HALINA. No.

Pause.

NEVILLE (*calmly*). You need never see me again.

HALINA. No.

NEVILLE (*staring at her*). You would rather take on the strength of the Immigration Service telling fantastic lies, than go through with this marriage.

HALINA. Yes. (*Pause.*) Don't take it personally again. (*Calmly.*) Please do not let it scrape your ego.

Silence.

You do want me to leave now, don't you?

Watching him.

You must, don't you? If you want me to, please tell me now.

Silence. They look at each other.

NEVILLE (*very precise tone*). You can stay on one condition.

HALINA (*turning*). And what is that?

NEVILLE. You let this mask drop.

HALINA. Mask? What do you mean?

NEVILLE. You've spent the whole time appearing confident, forcing yourself to be polite to people, being calm and enigmatic, spreading all this Slavic mist — you can't keep it up forever. (*He looks at her.*) It's driving me totally crazy.

Pause.

You have to let it out Halina — and this is the time to do it.

HALINA (*calmly*). You're giving me permission are you?

NEVILLE. Yes.

HALINA. To 'let it out'.

NEVILLE. Yes.

HALINA. You mean it?

NEVILLE (*very slight pause*). Yes.

HALINA moving towards Christmas tree.

HALINA. And you won't retract the permission, if I . . .

NEVILLE. No.

HALINA. I know, I'm sure (*Loud.*) I KNOW I CAN BEAT THEM.

Taking ball off Christmas tree.

If only giants are allowed in, then from the ordinary material that is my life I had to make at least one gigantic episode. And I *can* do it, use my brain for once. It's rusting from lack of use. When I'm at the interview I can't lose.

But — If they don't see me.

She breaks Christmas ball.

This incredible wait, every day passing and there's no news, the slowness of this country makes Poland seem a place of supersonic speed. (*She takes second ball off tree.*) They won't tell me when they'll see me.

NEVILLE (*nervously*). Careful Halina.

HALINA. Every time I call them. They are so polite, it is almost like they are caressing me with their apologies — and each time they delay just a little longer, just one more week closer to the deadline when I have to leave. It's like they are tearing your arm off, but one centimetre at a time.

Suddenly breaks the decorative balls on the tree, an assault on the Christmas tree, golden balls popping, as her frustration explodes.

It is the only way they can win — not letting me fight the first round.

NEVILLE. Leave something on the Christmas tree, if you possibly can.

HALINA. You did ask me (*She turns.*) I thought the permission covered everything.

The fury, the temper gives way to something very quiet and still. Outside the snow pouring down.

I was determined not to feel the usual conventional guilt on leaving one's country, leaving everyone behind, because if I did I was finished, and so far I've done very well. I *don't*.

Kneeling on floor, quiet.

But there is something else. I am a little afraid, I have a slight terror of being passed from country to country if I fail, being made stateless. A rotting package shovelled from one border to another, getting a little smaller each time, a piece coming off with every frontier, have you ever thought what that might be like — I haven't — with absolutely nowhere to go. Like falling into space, into the crack between land and sea.

She moves rhythmically backwards and forwards, NEVILLE *watching, not knowing what to do.*

Not just without a home, but with nowhere to *be.* Ending up in the last possible airport, surrounded by plastic bags.

Moving rythmically.

Don't get alarmed, I'm sorry, it'll pass quickly.

NEVILLE *staring across at her.*

NEVILLE. Halina.

HALINA (*quiet, calm*). It's going . . . bit by bit.

NEVILLE (*staring at her*). All this darkness coming out of you.

HALINA. I told you, don't worry.

NEVILLE (*moving cautiously up to her*). Halina, I don't know you very well, in fact I hardly know you at all . . . I'd like to *help* you — but how? (*Pause.*) I'm not sure what to say next (*Slight smile.*) very rare for me . . . because you're so determined, set on the wrong course of action.

You won't listen to reason. You don't know this country, you don't know your way around.

HALINA (*crunches final Christmas ball, lightly*). It's over, no problem now, it's all come out. No more to come.

NEVILLE (*watching her, intrigued*). Halina Rodziewizowna.

HALINA (*looking up*). Yes, (*Slight smile.*) you still pronounce it right.

HALINA *is smoking.*

NEVILLE. You're burning holes in the carpet.

HALINA. I didn't have permission for that?

NEVILLE. If you knew you were going to fail —

HALINA. I won't fail.

NEVILLE. But if you *did* know in advance you couldn't possibly succeed, and would damage yourself in trying — that they were never going to let you in because of your story.

HALINA. I might reconsider your plan. I don't know. Who knows!

NEVILLE. I see. (*Moving away.*) Don't worry. I know what to do next now, everything will become clear.

HALINA (*hardly listening*). I can't sleep, no point trying now, too much of the night has gone. It's snowing so hard, maybe they won't be able to get me out of the country, even if they want to. (*Moving to exit.*) I'll make a tremendous breakfast. A *Polish* breakfast.

NEVILLE. Is that wise?

HALINA (*detached*). You said you weren't going to make any Polish jokes.

She exits. Offstage she sings a fragment of a current English pop song.

NEVILLE. I have to make her see sense. (*Punching out number from diary, on phone.*) Come on — where is the tone? Typical of the Immigration Service, forget to check the tone is working on their answering machine.

He gets a connection.

NEVILLE. Right. (*His manner decisive, as if despatching some legal business.*) I have some information concerning Halina Rodziewizowna whose application for residency you received on December 12th.

Item one — she has been working illegally in the vicinity of Tottenham Court Road in a hi-fi and video store called the Sound Castle — without a work permit, or any authorisation, a simple check will reveal this.

Item two — her story of her dramatic ordeal in a Warsaw police station is a total fiction. The story is false, without foundation. If you now bother to look for any corroborative evidence, even a single witness, you will find none exist. That is the information I have. It is accurate. (*Signing off.*) An informed source. (*He rings off.*)

HALINA *singing off stage, fragment of song.*

I should have done that before. It's the only sensible course. She would never have brought it off, her way. (*Looking down at phone.*) My voice tangled up with all those others on the tape (*Sharp smile to himself.*) at least it's past the peak time for informing!

HALINA *enters with two mugs of steaming coffee.*

(*Turns.*) I've just been clearing things up here, Halina.

HALINA (*looking at cushions all over the floor*). So I see. (*She hands him the coffee.*) First course.

NEVILLE (*polite*). Thank you. That's good of you. Why were you singing such an odd song out there?

HALINA. It's very popular at the moment, didn't you know, it's sailing up the charts. (*Sings a fragment.*) I got a copy of it from the shop.

They stand watching the snow and the blue light breaking on the cyclorama, there is distant rumbling noise from outside.

NEVILLE. My God — it *is* almost morning.

HALINA. Neither of us will have slept tonight.

NEVILLE. I never heard that noise before, another one! I wonder what it is, distant thunder of snow ploughs setting out, spreading across London.

HALINA. Yes, the City's starting up again.

Blue light starting to break.

NEVILLE (*by window*). After what's happened these last few days, the sheer absence of logic, when the light comes up like now, I half expect to look out and see a different view there, a completely changed London. A fanciful whimsical mid-European version, full of eccentric deliberately perverse buildings, tilting at alarming angles and with perverse shaped people milling about across the square in the snow, old women with huge trunks on their backs and dwarves, all talking some incomprehensible language, which I can't reply to.

Light brightening all the time.

HALINA (*sipping coffee*). Well let's see what there is out there now.

As light increases.

You never know your luck do you.

Lights up to bright then blackout.

ACT TWO

Scene One

Sense of humming corridors in the blackout, of expectant noise, footsteps down the passage, foreign voices echoing and calling, phones ringing.

The mural, a mosaic of blue, green and silver stretching across the back wall where the cyclorama was.

Full expanse of the stage, bare except for a drinks machine and one chair.

The mural shows people arriving on a shore with blue and white water behind them, shadowy travellers facing an idealized glowing city on a hill, across an expanse of green.

Somebody has drawn one major piece of graffiti on the mural, a monster emerging out of the blue water with its teeth bared.

NEVILLE is upstage by a drinks machine, on the other side of the stage WAVENEY is standing, smoking with her back to him, she is wearing a red coat.

Downstage sitting on a chair is an old TURKISH WOMAN, scarf over her head, heavy boots and coat, and two large plastic bags bulging at her feet.

Bright early afternoon sun. As NEVILLE approaches machine, a deafening but totally unintelligible announcement booms out.

NEVILLE (*stopped in his tracks*). They've got a nice way of making you feel welcome here.

WAVENEY (*without turning round*). Yes.

NEVILLE *about to put money in,* TURKISH WOMAN *lifts her head shouts over to him, loud Turkish.*

NEVILLE. Yes. Quite. (NEVILLE *lifts his hand to put money in –* TURKISH WOMAN *calls out again.*)

WAVENEY. I think she knows something about that machine we don't. Maybe you should take her advice — it looks like she's spent rather a lot of time here.

NEVILLE. Yes, that's the feeling I get. (*To* TURKISH WOMAN.) Thank you. (*He smiles pleasantly.*) She's probably lost a large part of her life savings in that machine.

Bells ringing in distance.

NEVILLE (*to* WAVENEY). When's your interview?

WAVENEY. Not today. I hope. (*She turns to face him.*)

NEVILLE. I'm dreadfully sorry, I didn't recognise you, you're the girl from the shop. I thought you were one . . .

WAVENEY. So I see. Don't worry about it. (*Drily.*) Natural mistake.

NEVILLE (*smiles*). I was dazzled by this monstrous mural, people arriving somewhere . . . where do you think it's meant to be?

WAVENEY (*staring at the glowing city*). I don't know, maybe Southampton on a sunny day.

NEVILLE *smiles.*

WAVENEY. A nice place, wherever it is.

NEVILLE. Why are you here today?

WAVENEY. To give Halina a helping hand. (*Sharp.*) Why are you here?

ANDREW *enters briskly.*

ANDREW (*to* NEVILLE). There you are (*Glancing over his shoulder.*) I shouldn't be here of course.

NEVILLE. Why not?

ANDREW. I might be recognised, by either side. It's awash with people back there in the other section waiting for general interviews. There might be somebody there I failed to help — if they see me it could make the officers suspicious. (*Glancing around.*) It should be all right in this section. (*Worried.*) Where is Halina?

WAVENEY. She'll be here.

ANDREW (*hardly taking in* WAVENEY). She better be. We just got in under the wire before Christmas. Last Interviews today. (*Anxious.*) She'll be able to find it will she?

WAVENEY. She wouldn't miss this for the world.

NEVILLE (*breezily*). Yes. You know I never thought she'd get this far. That they'd actually see her about her story, I'm very surprised . . .

WAVENEY. Why?

NEVILLE. A reason of my own.

ANDREW (*looks at* WAVENEY). When's your interview?

WAVENEY. Not yet, not today.

NEVILLE. She's with us (*Slight smile.*) I think.

ANDREW (*surprised*). Really? A friend of Halina? (*Glances at the* TURKISH WOMAN.) People can wait months for special interviews, this looks like a good example. (*He smiles at the* TURKISH WOMAN.) At last the day has come.

NEVILLE (*smiles at* TURKISH WOMAN). Yes, she's had to wait outside these doors before.

TURKISH WOMAN *lifts head, she is near machine.*

NEVILLE. No, I'm not going to touch now, I assure you.

ANDREW (*pacing busily, pointing at mural*). This is interesting — like an illustration from a children's book. It's been through several important phases this building, first the strictly functional, just let's process the people without fuss and get the hell out of here.

Then, at the height of immigration the brutally unwelcoming, the benches so hard and so few of them, to flush out the people that weren't really serious about waiting for days without end. And now, for some bizarre reason, when there's practically no chance of ever getting into this country, they've decided to soften the place, murals, CHAIRS, we may even get some music . . .

HALINA *enters, she's wearing a lilac coat, a pale yellow hat, as if for a wedding.*

WAVENEY. She's here!

NEVILLE. My God, I didn't imagine you would dress like that!

HALINA. Why not?

NEVILLE. You look like the Queen Mother.

HALINA. Did you want me to wear black? That would have been a little predictable wouldn't it. (*She smiles.*) I thought I should try and surprise them. (*To* WAVENEY:) What do you think! I borrowed everything.

WAVENEY. I think you look just right.

HALINA. I'm glad you're here. I didn't think you'd be able to get away from the shop.

WAVENEY. That was easy. It's closed today for good. So I'm free.

HALINA. Really? Closed? As soon as that!

WAVENEY. Yes. (*Holding bag.*) This is full of spare parts! Hundreds of little leftovers from the shop!

HALINA (*rummaging in her bag with bits of plastic*). Yes, I've got some still, the ones I studied, I was going to give them back . . .

WAVENEY (*exuberant*). NO, NO! You might as well get something out of me losing my job! (*She smiles.*) I'm going to be your cheer leader today Halina.

ANDREW. Now I just want to issue a few guidelines.

HALINA. Guidelines?

ANDREW. Yes everything they say and do here has only one purpose, to prove you're *not what you make yourself out to be.*

HALINA. Yes.

ANDREW. That you're lying. Fraudulent. They may try any tack . . .

HALINA. Yes.

ANDREW. And be prepared for the extreme banality of the question

HALINA (*slight glance at* NEVILLE). I'm always prepared for that

ANDREW. Some officers favour the geographical approach, to find whether you're really a *native* of the country you say you are, it can be very blatant. (*To* HALINA:) For instance what is the highest range of mountains in Poland?

HALINA. I don't know. I have no idea.

NEVILLE. The Karkonosze, isn't it, in the Sudety mountains?

ANDREW. And the tallest individual mountain?

HALINA. I don't know. I'm sorry. I'm not very good on mountains. What about the cinemas and cafés of Warsaw?

NEVILLE. I should think it's Mount Sniezka.

HALINA (*looking at him*). That's very good.

ANDREW. It's strange, nobody ever knows the geography of their own country.

NEVILLE (*smiles*). Do you want the oldest churches in Warsaw? (*To* HALINA:) If I'd known we could have done some last-minute coaching.

ANDREW. Don't worry — the watchword must be consistency, either be consistently knowledgeable or consistently ignorant. Don't mix the two.

HALINA. I'll do my best not to.

ANDREW (*brisk*). I have to leave very soon. It's my perpetual fate to always have to exit before the *real* events occur, for obvious reasons, I could be recognised. So the final guidelines. . . . Aim for a clean interview.

WAVENEY. You mean no filthy jokes, won't that disappoint the

ANDREW. By which I mean don't be over-ambitious, you have to convince them of your worth, and the worth of your story. The best way . . .

BOOTH *appears wheeling a bicycle.*
ANDREW *immediately moves upstage.*

BOOTH (*stops*). Miss Rod, Rodz, Rodzi . . .

NEVILLE. Miss Rodziewizowna.

HALINA. Yes?

BOOTH (*holding out card*). Your number.

HALINA. What is it?

BOOTH. Number one.

HALINA. Good.

BOOTH. One, Six, Five, Zero.

HALINA *takes number.*

The size of the number is not necessarily of any significance. If you're called today you may bring only *one* friend in with you.

WAVENEY. Guess who that's going to be.

NEVILLE (*to* BOOTH). We understand. That will be me. I'm advising Miss Rodziewizowna.

BOOTH (*moving to leave*). And please try not to bring slush, snow, or mud into the office.

TURKISH WOMAN *calling after him, excuse, excuse me . . . he goes.*

ANDREW. Good we're making progress, we're into the first round.

WAVENEY (*to* TURKISH WOMAN). He'll return with your number, I'm sure, very soon.

TURKISH WOMAN *replying, excited, worried stream.*

NEVILLE (*indicating woman*). I've got it now, I think that's Turkish. (*Moving up to* HALINA.) Relax Halina, just relax, as much as possible.

HALINA (*very calmly*). I am.

NEVILLE (*animated*). You really are through to the interview you *realise.*

HALINA. I realise.

NEVILLE. No need to be nervous! (*Up to her.*) You know I was certain for a particular reason of my own, that you didn't have a chance in hell of reaching this stage, but that reason seems to have disappeared into thin air. It's evaporated. It's unrecorded! In fact, now you are here, I really want you to do well, Halina. I do. . . .

HALINA (*drily, slight smile*). That's good to know.

Blackout.

Scene Two

The wall of the office rolls across with a very large door in the middle of the wall.
    PEIRCE's *office now fills the stage. The door is oddly large for the scale of the walls. Around and above the door is misted glass looking out on the passages beyond, we can glimpse the mural on the back wall, now looking smudged and diffused through the glass.*
    There is a small picture on the wall of people on a golden beach mirroring the mural outside, it is the only ornament on the wall.
    The stage is very bare, just the desk with papers on it, and three chairs, one of them a very ordinary wooden chair, empty in the middle of the stage.
    PEIRCE *and* BOOTH *standing waiting,* NEVILLE *also in the office, they are looking towards the large open door.*
    HALINA *enters, looking confident almost flamboyant. She stops in the doorway.*

HALINA (*surveying* PEIRCE). So you're the one that's going to be seeing me.

PEIRCE. Miss Halina Rodziewizowna.

HALINA. Yes.

PEIRCE. I've pronounced it correctly?

NEVILLE. Yes.

PEIRCE (*looking across the stage at her*). If I may say so, you don't look at all like your photographs.

HALINA. Really. (*She smiles, still in doorway.*) I hope that will not be held against me, (*Glancing around.*) nor my choice of clothes.

PEIRCE (*welcoming smile*). I wouldn't have thought so. In this
    job I have to consume acres of newsprint, make sure I know
    what's happening out there. (*Indicates the outside.*) And I
    kept on coming across your picture.

HALINA. So did I. (*She smiles, moving forward.*) I quite enjoyed
    that in fact. Things travel very fast through your media.

She moves to wooden chair.

NEVILLE. This office has changed — it didn't look like this
    before.

*The chair HALINA is sitting on squeaks every time she moves,
rasping and rickety.*

PEIRCE (*invitingly*). Can we offer you anything Miss
    Rodziewizowna? There's some tea here, yes, and there's a
    single biscuit left.

HALINA. No. (*Lightly.*) I think I'll wait until I've got into the
    country, before I start becoming a serious tea drinker.

NEVILLE (*taking the biscuit*). Halina's a very cautious person.

PEIRCE. There is no mystery in what is going to happen — we're
    simply here to establish the truth. (*Pleasantly.*) Or to be more
    accurate what *I* think the truth is — that's all that matters.

HALINA. Good, that could not be clearer. (*Looking at him.*)
    Your impression of the truth.

PEIRCE (*lightly*). They're as many approaches in this building as
    there are interviewing officers. (*Moving to the desk.*) My
    colleague will not be saying anything, he is here merely to take
    notes.

PEIRCE *produces another full packet of biscuits from his
desk, he bites into one.*

PEIRCE. People have often been up all night before interviews,
    rehearsing.

HALINA. I promise not to fall asleep.

PEIRCE (*pleasantly*). And because they are nervous, lies can
    happen, sometimes almost by accident, and then people often
    seem to get into a spiral of untruths, which is unfortunately

disastrous, if I unpick one false link usually —

HALINA. The whole lot comes tumbling down — of course. (*She moves, rasping, squeak from the chair.*) And is this chair chosen on purpose? When people tense themselves up it squeaks. (*She does it, the chair squeaks.*) An English Lie Detector maybe? (*Slight smile.*) A very good idea.

PEIRCE (*watching her*). Like everything else in this building it's feeling its age. Miss Rodziewizowna, there is a fact about your case which you are probably unaware of.

NEVILLE. Which is what?

PEIRCE (*calmly*). We have received certain information about you — alternative information, via a phone call to this building.

NEVILLE. You mean somebody informed on her!

PEIRCE. Yes.

HALINA (*blowing smoke from small cigar*). How strange — somebody bothering to give false information about *me*.

NEVILLE. I hope having mentioned it — you are going to tell us exactly what it consists of, and where it came from?

PEIRCE. The information was anonymous — which we take much less seriously, what this person didn't realise is, we get a torrent of malicious false information, as well as the truth.

NEVILLE. Obviously this must all be withdrawn — I demand on Miss Rodziewizowna's behalf, these anonymous allegations be erased from the case.

PEIRCE (*ignoring him, to* HALINA). It merely makes this difference — before I was under pressure from those I'm answerable to, to make this interview a formality because of all the publicity, and the nature of that publicity. That can no longer be the case.

NEVILLE. No, I must *insist* you disregard these flagrantly malicious allegations.

HALINA *moving, chair rasping.*

HALINA. The chair's getting excited. Please, I can't make you forget whatever you've been told — so I'll just have to demonstrate it's not true.

PEIRCE (*looking at papers*). Your preliminary questionnaire — your answers seem very satisfactory, very clear, your education, the sudden halt, not married, no children, your father's loss of power and your time looking after him.

HALINA (*lightly*). 29 years.

PEIRCE. 29 years, yes, a long time. Your interests . . . by the way have you bought any records since you arrived here?

HALINA (*meeting his eyes, smiles*). You mean gramophone records to play on a gramophone?

PEIRCE. Obviously.

HALINA (*stretching her legs out*). I have been listening to the radio like a small child, all channels, it's started to grow on my ear . . . No I haven't.

PEIRCE. You've never been into a record shop!

HALINA. I didn't say that, I've wandered into a few.

PEIRCE (*effortlessly, casually*). What have you done since you arrived here, what jobs?

NEVILLE. She hasn't.

HALINA (*cutting him off*). I haven't a job, it's illegal isn't it. I see now you ask an innocent question and then slide one underneath, the one with the kick. (*She smiles.*) That's good.

PEIRCE. You haven't worked in a store selling hi-fi video equipment?

HALINA (*calm smile*). If I'd been offered such a job I might have been tempted (NEVILLE *twitches.*) but I wasn't.

I know nothing about hi-fi. (*Casually.*) You've checked of course!

PEIRCE (*briskly*). Yes. The stores we contacted, none of them had ever heard of you.

He looks at her.

Miss Rodziewizowna — I think I want to move straight to

your story, your dramatic story.

HALINA (*smoking small cigar*). Good, I have been waiting for this.

PEIRCE. Because the merit of your application so clearly depends on that. (*Looking down at notes.*) I see you were picked up by the police while speeding . . .

HALINA. No. (*Calm smile.*) You are quite wrong right from the beginning. We were 'picked up' while driving normally late one evening. We were taken to the police station in Karmelicka Street . . . (*The chair squeaks.*) One of the legs of this chair is vibrating . . .

> HALINA *continues talking effortlessly as she gets up and changes the chair for the one* BOOTH *is sitting on.*

There were five of us, we were told there was something wrong with the license of the car. At first we were put in this normal room in the police station. Excuse me (BOOTH *forced to vacate his chair, she takes his.*) Thank you . . . which even had magazines on the table, (*She sits on new chair.*) that's better, we sat there for . . .

PEIRCE. What are the colours of the walls in this room?

HALINA. The walls? A pale green.

PEIRCE. You remember it just like that, you didn't have to think.

HALINA (*leaning back on new chair*). You know for a fact, or you ought to, I was in that police station — so obviously I know the colour of the walls, what you want to prove or disprove is what happened there. (*Innocently.*) Isn't it?

NEVILLE (*coolly*). Do you want Miss Rodziewizowna to continue or not?

PEIRCE. Very much.

HALINA (*very casual smoking cigar*). In fact there was a picture of the American movie ET on the walls with its feet sticking out. I hope we can leave the walls now. The youngest of the guards then came in, he said we all had to come down

the passage with him, I thought they must want to take
photographs of us, I even looked at myself in the mirror.

PEIRCE. What were the exact words he used, this young guard?

HALINA (*brushing this aside*). I don't remember — some things
I remember, some I don't. We found outselves at the end of
the passage, in a large old washroom full of baths, that were
unused, dead.

PEIRCE (*incredulous*). Baths?

HALINA. Yes, *Baths,* you know that you wash in; the taps were
rusted up, I remember seeing some spiders at the bottom.
Suddenly one of the guards shouted, 'Take off your shoes.
Take them off now'. We all did.

PEIRCE. You were barefoot now, by these baths.

HALINA. No, it was *winter,* as you know. I was wearing blue
tights. (*She smokes calmly.*) An old more senior police
guard came in, he started shrieking at us, we had been
found guilty, crimes against the state, they had checked our
files, we were the ones they had been searching for, they had
proof, at last they'd found us. (*She turns to* BOOTH.) Please
be quiet on that chair of yours, if possible.

She looks back at PEIRCE.

I thought they were drunk, this being New Year's Eve.

PEIRCE (*casually*). And you were all standing in this old
decaying kitchen?

HALINA. No, the *washroom.* Please *try* to listen. (*She pauses,
flicking the ash off her stubby cigar.*) We were taken outside,
which was brightly lit, with very high walls, a small pond in
the middle, with two large goldfish swimming in it, I
remember thinking there's hardly any room for them in the
pond. We were told to go over to the far end of the courtyard.

PEIRCE (*sensing an opening*). These fat goldfish in *winter,*
Miss Rodziewizowna, this pond in fact was frozen solid of
course, wasn't it!

HALINA. *NO,* there was a pipe running into it. Please remember

Warsaw is often no colder than London. (*Tone changing to firm.*) I will go on, we were lined up against the wall, arranged carefully, we were forbidden to turn round. They stopped shouting, there was a curious silence (*Perfectly matter-of-fact.*) I heard this click behind us, and there was a moment, a very clear moment of realisation, then of panic, almost like a blow punching you in the stomach — they were going to shoot us. We . . .

PEIRCE. One moment Miss Rodziewizowna. Did you turn round, at this moment?

HALINA (*momentary pause*). I'm trying to remember the exact order, yes, the lights were shining in my eyes.

People started screaming, then somebody dropped their spectacles, there were three men behind us with machine guns, they were yelling at us this abuse, both maniacally and then very deliberately and all this time, there was this song playing on a radio from somewhere, a Polish pop song of that Christmas, a really banal song.

Then suddenly they started whispering to each other, the police, and said they had decided to select only half of us, we —

BOOTH. Could you say that again, I didn't get that.

HALINA (*sweeping this aside*). IF this is a device — it's not a very clever one, get someone who can take shorthand properly next time.

We were led back, into a different room, a long low room, and there.

She gets up, having seemed very casual she shifts gear, now with full authority.

This is the very clever thing they did, their one stroke of genuine imagination, one of the most alarming things I've ever seen, there was this pile of clothes in the corner, other people's clothes, shoes, stockings, spectacles, even false teeth, in these heaps, and all over the floor these buttons staring up at you.

We all thought of course, this must be the group before us,

they had been shot, we really believed it was real then. (*She moves.*) *No,* don't interrupt.

Four times, *four* times they took us out there, and put us through that, (*Loud.*) until there was *nothing* left inside us, *nothing,* and the final selection had been made. And I was in it, I was one of the chosen, come through this door they said, come through, and we did, we went though — only to find ourselves out in the street, and free.

Pause.

PEIRCE (*drily*). I see.

HALINA (*lightly*). We never got our shoes back either.

The door flies open, the TURKISH WOMAN *holding her bags, asking excitedly looking for her interview.*

PEIRCE (*immediately*). Not in here, your interview's not in here . . . along the corridor . . . you'll find your officer somewhere else.

She nods and leaves with her bags.

(*To* HALINA:) It must have been an ordeal Miss Rodziewizowna.

HALINA. It was yes.

PEIRCE (*sharp*). Having to tell me all that.

NEVILLE. Of course it was.

HALINA (*having been wrong footed, recovering immediately*). No, not really, it was all right. There's even a certain pleasure in retelling something you've survived. I've told it so much in the last few weeks it just comes out now. (*Looks at him.*) And you *listened,* in the end.

NEVILLE. I feel now we should —

PEIRCE (*sharp at* NEVILLE). Please, be quiet. (*To* HALINA, *watching her closely*:) You complained of course about this appalling event.

HALINA. Two days later, the official response was — it never happened. And when I got in touch with the others who went through it with me, they'd all been let go that morning, they didn't want to talk about any of it, or even hear it mentioned.

After my official complaint, I never felt entirely safe again, from the police.

PEIRCE. Not entirely safe.

HALINA. No. That is why I'm here. Before you ask I think the reason it happened was a kind of manic spite from the guards, revenge for bad publicity, or simple terrible boredom.

Pause, PEIRCE *watching her.*

PEIRCE. That seems conceivable, yes.

HALINA (*to* BOOTH). Can I see your notes please, you can have your seat back in a minute. (*As she flicks through* BOOTH's *notes.*)

(*To* PEIRCE:) Something I don't understand if you want to prove I'm lying, you don't have to prove anything, you just *tell* them that I am.

(*Pleasantly, turning to* BOOTH, *with his notes:*) These aren't too good, no, a little imprecise you've missed some detail — I'll correct them later for you.

(*Innocently looks up at* PEIRCE.) What's next please?

PEIRCE *suddenly exits sharply, frustrated movement,* BOOTH *scurrying behind him.*

Round one. Reasonable.

Blackout.

Scene Three

HALINA *and* WAVENEY *alone on stage in* PEIRCE's *office, with the large door wide open and the vista of the mural seen through it. Warm mid-afternoon sun, distant music, dance music drifting from the bowels of the building, mingled with the announcements for interviews booming out.* WAVENEY *stands in the open doorway, back to the audience, staring towards the music.*

WAVENEY. Listen to that! Can you imagine anything worse than a Christmas party full of immigration officers? All trying to work out who in the room hasn't been invited. (*She turns smiling.*) I wouldn't like to try to gatecrash that party!

HALINA. Maybe that's why they haven't come back — they are dancing with each other down there.

WAVENEY. They'll be back for more, don't worry! I've lost count of the times I've been stopped out there (*Indicates through door.*) given a number, and told to wait for my interview. If I'm here any longer I'll start wanting to tell an officer my life story.

HALINA. He doesn't believe me yet Waveney, I can feel it.

WAVENEY. He believes you, you are doing well.

HALINA. How do you know?

WAVENEY. It's being relayed out there, live coverage, another giant screen, people are crowding round to see, betting on the outcome! No, you're doing fine — you're still here aren't you.

HALINA. He's fifty-fifty. Sometimes I think I've got him, and then he gets away from me. There's too little room for error.

WAVENEY. I don't know why I want you so much to get in, but I do you know. Badly.

HALINA. I had noticed.

WAVENEY. There's nothing at all logical about it. (*Sharp smile.*) Maybe I wouldn't mind somebody I know winning something for once. (*She moves.*) So don't let me down.

HALINA. Thank you! (*Looking down at her hands as she smokes.*) I don't want to smoke too much. (*Lightly.*) I want to unnerve him with a dizzy calm. (*She fiddles with plastic bits in her bag.*)

WAVENEY. You will! (*Moving loudly to wall where plaster has come away.*) Look at this — the 'gate-way' to the country is falling to pieces! I don't know why I feel things so extremely today, of all days, vividly.

It must be having to be out there in those passages, I keep getting twinges in them, bits of smells, bits of the floor, bring back memories.

HALINA. Yes, official passages affect me like that too. You feel absolutely nothing's secure, not even the lineoleum under your feet, trap doors suddenly might spring open.

WAVENEY. My first few days in this country a lot of it was spent in passages like those back there, about our papers. The *waiting* started right here, I was clinging to my mother, I was only four, everything was so blotchy and pale, I kept on not being able to work out the expression on people's faces, they were just blanks and blobs bending towards me.

HALINA. I've been having that problem over these last few weeks — and I am not four years old!

WAVENEY. Even the first racist remarks I ever heard came spitting out of this bland round pebble of a face.

And I remember when I was staring out of the bus window, coming in from the airport, the day we arrived. I saw these people working in their gardens, they must have been wearing very pale clothes because they looked completely *nude,* and I thought how odd, all these people must go naked in this country all the time, even though it's so cold, will I have to? (*She really laughs.*) I don't think anybody's first impression of here has ever been more wrong!

NEVILLE *enters holding tray with paper cups on it.*

NEVILLE. Here! Some drink.

HALINA. At last. (*Her head goes back, drinking deeply.*)

NEVILLE (*smiles*). It's tap water. I avoided all the machines. (*Looking at* WAVENEY.) I think the rules maybe being broken — there are at this precise moment, three of us together in this room.

WAVENEY *not moving.*

HALINA (*as she drinks*). No sign of them?

NEVILLE. No, they've gone away to regroup obviously.

WAVENEY (*indicating* HALINA *drinking*). They're being towelled down in their corner, and you in yours.

HALINA. Yes.

NEVILLE (*very animated*). I can tell you Halina, it's an extraordinary sensation when you're listening to someone telling a story who you know is *lying.*

WAVENEY (*sharp*). Don't use that word here — what do you think you're doing?

NEVILLE (*ignoring this*). First reaction — nobody, but nobody is going to believe this, stop! Just tell as little as possible. I wanted to go up and gag you, shout keep it simple for Godsake! And you were so outrageously casual, I thought she wants to get into this country so much and this is the best she can do — but then (*Pause.*) it really did begin to sound not at all bad.

HALINA. Given time, is that going to grow into a compliment?

NEVILLE. Maybe. There were too many details of course, the goldfish were severely unnecessary, but it was a skilful mixture, aimed accurately at several nerve-ends, traces of Kafka, a touch of cheap cold-war thrillers, from all that reading you've done (*Moves, indicating building.*) it should appeal to people here, on the edge of being too much but not quite.

WAVENEY. I think it's really irresponsible of you to talk like this — why the hell don't you stop it?

NEVILLE. What for? You're not suggesting they've bugged this room?

HALINA. I don't think this particular one would want to bug — it would take all the skill and art out of his job.

NEVILLE (*moving over to* HALINA). Anyway we have to concentrate on what they're planning next for you?

HALINA. I wish they'd come back!

WAVENEY (*calling across*). And why don't you leave her alone — I think she can look after herself you know.

NEVILLE. I have no idea why you're being so hostile.

WAVENEY. Don't you?

NEVILLE. You don't even know me.

WAVENEY. I know enough.

Noises ringing, WAVENEY *moves to the door.*

NEVILLE (*turning*). It has noises all its own this building. (*To* HALINA:) Now, please don't over do it this round, don't allow yourself to be tempted, you'll forget what you've said and they'll trip you up.

HALINA (*quiet*). Yes, Neville.

NEVILLE (*lightly*). And have *some* grace under pressure — you have to persuade them you're worth having remember. (*He smiles.*) At least you have undoubtedly achieved one thing already — the informing has been neutralised, wiped off the record — totally annihilated!

WAVENEY. Informing? Who's been informing on you?

HALINA. They won't tell us.

PEIRCE *and* BOOTH *moving into doorway.*

WAVENEY. The terrible duo — are they going to hand out parking tickets because there are three of us in the room at the same time?

Noise of voices, music and bells as PEIRCE *and* BOOTH *move into room.*

PEIRCE. I would like now, if possible, just to have a word alone with our friend here.

NEVILLE. Me? Of course. Absolutely. (*To* HALINA *and* WAVENEY.) Just leave us alone for a moment could you.

HALINA (*sharp*). Why is it necessary to talk to him?

NEVILLE (*confidently*). Yes, just step outside, I won't be long. (*To* HALINA:) It's time to do business, I'll be with you in a minute.

WAVENEY. Aren't either of us allowed to stay in here — and keep an eye on him.

NEVILLE (*smoothly*). No, no it's best if we do this on our own, settle up — OK!

HALINA *and* WAVENEY *exit,* HALINA *taking a look back at the door.*

PEIRCE *and* BOOTH *stand together.*

NEVILLE. As you can see, she is patently telling the truth.

PEIRCE (*looking at his papers*). Mr . . .

NEVILLE. If you are concerned about the publicity, we can do a deal about that — there'll be no press release from us saying she's been granted residency.

PEIRCE. Sit down please, Mr Gregory.

NEVILLE (*amused smile*). You want me to sit down? Of course.

He sits on the wooden chair centre stage.

PEIRCE. You don't mind helping us for a moment?

BOOTH. Just one thing we want to ask you.

PEIRCE. Why are you here?

NEVILLE (*smiling confident*). Why am *I* here?

PEIRCE. Wouldn't you say it's a little odd someone like you representing a . . .

NEVILLE (*interrupting pleasantly*). It's not odd, I am a solicitor who happened to meet Miss Rodziewizowna, and is giving her free advice.

PEIRCE (*sharp*). But you work for a firm specialising in the entertainment industry.

NEVILLE. Yes — but before then I worked in a general inner-city practice, I encountered every conceivable problem — like you do here.

BOOTH. And why did you leave?

NEVILLE. Survival.

PEIRCE. You mean money.

NEVILLE (*expansively, one professional to another*). No — the money was about the same, but I began not to be able to cope with them all. Everything suddenly started to multiply wildly, you must know the feeling. These worried faces spattering the walls with their problems, shuffling in everyday, full of rage and grievance before they even get up to my desk, sometimes with tiny problems that had grown inside their head — other times with problems so heavy they weighed on *you* the whole week. (*He smiles.*) I found I couldn't help them so I moved on.

Dipping about in copyright law is a little less interesting though.

BOOTH. How would you categorize your involvement in this case?

NEVILLE. Categorize! I don't know why you're so interested. I am advising Miss Rodziewizowna, I was introduced to her by a friend.

BOOTH. Who was this friend?

NEVILLE. The friend? (*About to say, then stops himself.*) An acquaintance, a woman who happened to.

PEIRCE (*suddenly*). A woman! What's her name?

NEVILLE (*brushing this aside*). Why do you want to know her name — she only introduced us, it is irrelevant, there is absolutely no need for me to give you her name.

BOOTH. So you would categorize your involvement as one of polite interest?

NEVILLE (*effortlessly*). Determined to have your category aren't you, concerned, detached interest.

PEIRCE (*sharp*). You're *living* with Miss Rodziewizowna.

NEVILLE. I am not 'living' with her.

BOOTH. She's staying in your house.

NEVILLE. Yes — she's staying in my house because she had nowhere else to go.

BOOTH. Nowhere else to go!

NEVILLE. That's right. (*Thinking quickly.*) When she decided to go public with her story — she didn't feel secure where she was before. I expect you now want to know the colour of the walls in the house.

PEIRCE. No, we know that.

Face appearing of the TURKISH WOMAN *staring through the fan shaped window above the door, directly above* NEVILLE's *chair. Her face staring down at him watching, occasionally mouthing something.*

NEVILLE. What is she doing looking in here?

PEIRCE (*hardly looking up*). Don't take any notice — they stick like limpets at this time of year, when we're closing down for the holiday.

BOOTH. Where does your family originally come from Mr Gregory?

NEVILLE (*startled by the question*). Originally come from? I have no idea. (*Then confident smile.*) Luton, I think.

BOOTH. Luton where?

NEVILLE (*staring in disbelief*). Luton, England, do you know of any others?

PEIRCE. Were both your parents English? No foreign connections? No foreign blood?

NEVILLE. Of course. I'm wholly English. (*Sharp smile.*) What the hell is this?

WAVENEY *staring down with the* TURKISH WOMAN *through the window, later joined by three or four other faces gathering to watch, a cluster of faces watching him on the chair, through the glass.*

BOOTH. How long have you been in this country?

NEVILLE. How long? I have lived here all my life.

BOOTH. And where were you born?

NEVILLE (*loud*). Born?

PEIRCE. It's not necessary to repeat the question!

NEVILLE. In India.

BOOTH. In India!

NEVILLE. Yes — my father was a minor official in the

diplomatic service, who was sacked for chronic unpunctuality. So he started selling cars, extremely successfully. Back here in the old country of course.

And now — I have no idea what you two think you're playing at, but I'm moving this on to other matters, Halina is waiting to . . .

BOOTH (*pronouncing his name with a foreign lilt*). And it is your belief Mr Gregori, that your parents are wholly British?

NEVILLE (*flicking this away*). My mother, not that it's anything to do with you, was half Belgian.

BOOTH *makes an 'aha' noise.*

What's more you know (*To* PEIRCE:) you've broken your word — you said this character here (*Pointing to* BOOTH.) was not going to say anything, he'd be a silent notetaker — but he keeps piping up, asking idiotic questions.

PEIRCE (*standing facing him from desk*). He asks the bread and butter questions — I ask the interesting ones.

BOOTH. Your parents Mr Gregor *i.*

NEVILLE (*swinging round, very sharp*). My God — I have no other foreign blood whatever! I'm British. I'm fucking English for Godsake. (*Pause.*) You're going to ask me for my passport next!

PEIRCE. And it is your belief that your parents were married at the time you were born?

NEVILLE (*savage smile*). These questions are rapidly becoming objectionable as well as ludicrous. Have you two gone out of your tiny minds? I'm Miss Rodziewizowna's advisor.

BOOTH. A little chipping away and we find you're not quite as wholly British as you make yourself out to be. It's so often the way with people who think themselves so English, scrape away the surface. . . .

NEVILLE. *I'm* not applying for anything, you idiots, I live here!

PEIRCE (*calmly*). You don't have to answer any of our

questions of course Mr Gregory, but that may not help your
client.

NEVILLE (*ebullient, ridiculing them as he moves*). It's a
wonderful thought isn't it, a true paranoid's fantasy, some
innocent wanders in here to help a friend and ends up being
deported himself! (*Inspired by his own thought.*) Anybody
who happens to come into this building, the place closes
round you, and you have to explain your whole existence.
(*Pointing out* PEIRCE *and* BOOTH.) Suddenly you two take a
look at these perfectly respectable people, does he justify the
place he takes up, is he worth keeping? (*Mimics.*) 'I've reason
to believe you are no longer entitled to stay in this country
owing to your irredeemable mediocrity?' (*Looking at them.*)
I can think of a great many candidates!

(*He stops.*) Shall we now return to serious subjects?

PEIRCE. Sit down and calm down Mr Gregory. I simply want to
establish your motive for being here, which I don't
understand.

NEVILLE *pointing up at the collection of faces,* WAVENEY
and the TURKISH WOMAN *looking down at him through the
fan shaped window.*

NEVILLE. And is that a public gallery now, are you selling
tickets! What the hell are they doing up there watching me.

PEIRCE. The corridors have been re-routed because of
redecoration – take no notice of them.

The faces staring down. The sun has gone a late afternoon red.

BOOTH. Have you ever been behind the Iron Curtain?

NEVILLE (*to* PEIRCE). You were right – he certainly does ask
predictable questions, the answer is yes.

BOOTH. Where Mr Gregori?

NEVILLE. I have spent a week in Czechoslovakia as a tourist.

BOOTH. Czechoslovakia! And that's all Mr Gregori, no Polish
connections?

NEVILLE. What is this Greg *ori* shit – No, I have never been to

Poland, nor Russia, nor surprisingly Afghanistan.

PEIRCE. Do you speak Russian?

NEVILLE (*to* PEIRCE, *sarcastic*). *That's* an interesting question! Yes 'O' level Russian and I also have to confess I once went to a Bulgarian movie.

Faces staring down, he gets up.

NEVILLE. I am now bringing this part of the interview to a close. It is over.

He moves the chair upstage and places it firmly against wall, smiling and shaking his head.

I love the idea! Being evicted from one's own country, escorted to the airport with just a toothbrush and pushed out!

PEIRCE (*watching him*). You work Mr Gregory, are you happy with your work, your job?

NEVILLE (*surprised*). My work, of course, yes.

BOOTH. I thought you said it didn't interest you. (NEVILLE *turns round.*) You *did* say that, didn't you?

PEIRCE (*before he has time to answer*). The firm doing well is it?

NEVILLE. Yes, very.

PEIRCE. And you?

NEVILLE *standing in the middle of the stage.*

NEVILLE. Me!

PEIRCE. Yes, your position inside the firm, how successful would you say *you* were.

NEVILLE. That of course is none of your business at all, but as it happens things are going very well, extremely well in fact.

PEIRCE. A large firm isn't it. (*Idly.*) Several lawyers of around your age, what if I were to suggest to you that they were about to let you go?

NEVILLE (*incredulous at this, then white with fury*). That's a *complete* lie! That's a total fiction!

PEIRCE. Knowing how competitive these firms have to be in the present climate, would it surprise you to find that they are seriously thinking of dispensing with your. . . .

NEVILLE. That is *not* true!

BOOTH. How can they keep on somebody that's not interested in their job?

NEVILLE (*loud*). You're guessing, this is totally malicious and unfounded, to unnerve me, just grubby innuendo, which I refuse —

BOOTH (*cutting him off*). Can you tell us Mr Gregori as of this moment are you considered *necessary*.

NEVILLE. Necessary? Necessary where?

BOOTH. At your job. All things considered, in the end, *Are you necessary*?

NEVILLE. I will of course be making an official complaint about this.

BOOTH (*very loud, bearing down on him*). ARE YOU NECESSARY OR NOT?

Pause.

BOOTH. You're not necessary are you.

NEVILLE (*forced to reassure himself*). Yes of course I'm necessary. Very necessary. There is no doubt about that.

Faces staring down.

PEIRCE. You are naturally aware that it is a criminal offence to aid and abet someone to enter this country under false pretences. If a member of the legal profession was involved, they might never . . .

NEVILLE. How *dare* you try to do this, how dare you subject me to these insane questions. (*Shouting, pointing.*) Whoever heard of an interview taking place watched like a squash match by that gallery of ghouls and weirdos up there. It is totally irregular and surreal! I reject *everything* that's happened here.

BOOTH (*with notes*). We have so far, you were born in India,

with Belgian parents, you speak Russian, you have travelled
behind the Iron Curtain, you may be about to lose your

NEVILLE (*incandescent with rage*). I utterly deplore this attempt
to create a crude destablising situation (*Loud.*) I want this
recorded! This despicable attempt to undermine my status so
I will reveal something about Halina. (*Pointing.*) I'm going to
get you two for this! I promise you, you've had it —
absolutely. You're finished. I am now going to summon Miss
Rodziewizowna (*Calling.*) Halina, Halina. (*Moving.*) You may
ask me no further questions, you have absolutely no right —

PEIRCE. Allow me to be the Judge of that. There is something
that troubles me about you Mr Gregory and has been from
the first moment I met you. Why.

NEVILLE (*completely enraged, picking up chair*). This discussion
is *terminated*! It is *concluded*! (*With chair.*) You cannot
threaten me or question me — I forbid you to make any
remarks about my future or my employment, which you know
nothing about . . . (*Shouting, waving chair.*) this has to stop
right now, or there'll be really ugly consequences, I warn you,
I WARN you.

HALINA *standing in doorway.*

NEVILLE *holding the chair out in front of him,* PEIRCE *and*
BOOTH *facing him.*

PEIRCE. Miss Rodziewizowna?

HALINA (*to* NEVILLE). I see you are getting on just fine.

She moves into the room.

It's all right Neville — I will handle this.

Blackout.

Scene Four

Bells, and cacophony of voices, giving way to party music.
PEIRCE's *office a few minutes later.*

Christmas lights have come on around the mural on the back wall.

Dark outside, the sun going down rapidly. Behind the blind covering the window in the side wall, orange neon blinks from a sign outside. And heavy institutional lamps have come on above their heads.

HALINA, NEVILLE *and* WAVENEY *facing* PEIRCE *and* BOOTH. *Christmas party music and noise of laughter really gets going as scene progresses, wafting towards them.*

PEIRCE. Do we have the key?

BOOTH (*staring straight at* HALINA *and* NEVILLE). The key?

PEIRCE. Yes to this . . . (*Indicating bottom drawer of desk.*)
It's Christmas. (*He smiles.*) People tell me. Let us have some sherry Alan. (*Indicates* BOOTH *to unlock cupboard.*)
Everybody steals in this building, so let's hope there's a bottle still there.

HALINA. I think we'd rather have a decision than a drink.

NEVILLE. Yes. (*Very sharp.*) If that's not asking too much.

BOOTH *serving sherry.*

PEIRCE. Mr Gregory and I were just having a relaxed chat in here, I was taking a short cut, a holiday indulgence, a little horseplay. Something about Mr Gregory bothers me — but no hard feelings I hope.

NEVILLE. Why don't you just cut the crap and tell us what you're thinking.

WAVENEY. And going to do?

PEIRCE (*casually*). Haven't I told you that? (*Moving by desk.*)
There is just one thing that still worries me.

HALINA. Just one, I thought there were many many more.

PEIRCE. Your story convinces me — except for one small thing.

HALINA (*moving along wall*). Yes?

PEIRCE. Snow, darkness, a courtyard . . . a mock-execution, people up against the wall knowing they are going to die, there is an echo going on in my head, a sense of recognition, the Russian novelist Fyodor Dostoevsky with whom you are no doubt familiar, the same thing happened to him, the mock execution, thinking he was going to die in the snow.

NEVILLE. I don't recall this, I think you are —

PEIRCE (*sharp*). You knew the story and borrowed it, made it your own.

HALINA (*stopping, turning*). *That* is what you're worrying about.

PEIRCE. Yes.

HALINA. Just that?

BOOTH. Yes.

HALINA (*watching them*). You're *right*. (*Pause. Very controlled.*) I have memories of the story — it would be difficult for me to come here and tell you of any example of arbitrary cruelty which did not have some parallel, the banality of the minds of the people who do such acts means they must often imitate each other. (*She smiles.*) There are no exclusive rights, no copyright on any one method. Anyway it happened to me, and possibly to Dostoevsky — I think that is probably the only thing that we have in common. (*Lightly, looking straight at him.*) Though you never know.

PEIRCE (*not taking his eyes off her*). That is your explanation? (*Loud.*) Alan! Could you leave us please.

BOOTH *looks startled.*

And try to get rid of the last stragglers.

BOOTH (*slight smile at door*). See you again, Mr Gregori.

BOOTH *opens the door, the* TURKISH WOMAN *standing there, stammering 'I've missed my interview, it's gone, it is too late now, they won't give me another . . . please find me another one'* BOOTH *ushers her away.*

PEIRCE (*as* BOOTH *closes door*). I think it's beginning to grate on him, still being a nuts and bolts man. (*Turning sharply.*) You're right of course Miss Rodziewizowna.

HALINA. I am?

PEIRCE (*suddenly, sitting informally on desk*). I'm sometimes offered two examples of the same grotesque experience from totally different parts of the world, on a single day.

HALINA. Exactly, yes.

PEIRCE (*orange neon behind him*). People come in here some-times, with the most appalling stories, you listen to these terrible details, and then you walk out of these doors into the bland streets of Croydon, a lukewarm London evening, red buses blundering by, and even after several years, the contrast is for a moment extremely sharp and vivid.

WAVENEY. What's he playing at?

PEIRCE (*serious*). Miss Rodziewizowna — this is a firm request. Please sit down.

HALINA *sits centre stage.*

I have to tell you, I am inclined, I think I have to believe you, and *will* recommend your application is accepted.

HALINA (*immediately jumping up from chair*). You will? You have!

WAVENEY. You've done it.

NEVILLE. Is this absolutely definite? We have the right to assume this is the final —

PEIRCE. You may have elaborated a little here and there, people seem unable to resist, like a corridor is in reality bright pink — but they think that sounds too cheerful so they make it brown, the colour of excrement.

HALINA. The walls really matter to you don't they!

PEIRCE. But I believe you.

HALINA. I don't dare open my mouth in case I push things the wrong way again.

NEVILLE. That's very wise.

HALINA (*suddenly it really hits her*). YOU BELIEVE ME? HE BELIEVES ME!

PEIRCE (*loud, injured tone*). NO! You mustn't think of leaving yet.

NEVILLE *has already moved to door.*

One has so little chance to get to know people in this job. (*His legs go up on his desk.*)

WAVENEY (*whispering*). Don't relax . . . don't relax.

PEIRCE. Sudden intense meetings and then nothing. I have a feeling there are some cheese balls here somewhere. (*Pulling open a drawer.*) Completely off the record — when I recommend against people, I have no idea what is going to happen to them.

HALINA. No you can't, how could you?

PEIRCE (*his tone suddenly personal, opening up,* HALINA *never taking her eyes off him for a moment*). I could be sending them back to a very uncertain future, I have an image of these people orbiting the world, going from frontier to frontier, desperately trying to find anyone who will let them in.

HALINA. I feel terribly lucky, I can tell you.

PEIRCE (*leaning forward*). And you know sometimes I'm interviewing somebody, and a hand, a gesture, a certain phrase jolts the mind, makes it compute backwards and I realise I've seen this person under another name, another passport, another identity, years before.

HALINA. How awful! For both of you!

WAVENEY (*cynical smile*). It's a very difficult job what you've got, we know.

PEIRCE. Yes, you have to budget for people's innate creativity, their unpredictability, the endless variations in how they are going to lie.

There is the sound of an alarm bell, hooters suddenly clammering, PEIRCE *uncoils his legs.*

PEIRCE. That is my summons, the typical greeting from one officer to another! (*He smiles.*) I hate this time, the dregs of the year. I have to try and face the terrible prospect of the Christmas party, can you imagine anything worse than a party full of immigration officers?

HALINA *laughs spontaneously, as does* WAVENEY.

(*Smiles.*) Yes, lots of bad jokes about the passengers, about rats scrabbling to get on a sinking ship, all my colleagues, dancing wearing party hats!

PEIRCE *smiles, leans forward casually and touches* HALINA'*s knee.*

By the way what's that you've been playing with during the interview, I've been trying to work it out?

HALINA. This? (*Automatically, holding plastic box.*) It's a Nagoaka moving permalloy stereo cartridge – MP 30 XX.

PEIRCE. Really? Nagoaka.

HALINA. Yes, moving perm – (*She stops.*)

Music in the silence.

(*In Polish.*) Oh my God.

Her head goes down, sudden shout in Polish.

PEIRCE. Yes – a small but vital item of hi-fi equipment.

HALINA'*s head goes back, another shout.*

NEVILLE (*loud*). Just something she picked up in my flat, I have lots of spare equipment lying around (*Loud.*) it means absolutely nothing!

WAVENEY. I gave it to her just now it's mine – she knows nothing about it.

HALINA. *Please* – don't, there is no point in doing that now, he knows that was a bad mistake.

WAVENEY. Something told me you weren't safe – not until you were out of this building.

PEIRCE. Miss Rodziewizowna is about to admit she worked in this country illegally.

HALINA (*answers in Polish*).

Pause.

You will have to settle for it in Polish. Undone by a gramophone needle! I can't believe I was so stupid.

NEVILLE. What are you doing with this absurd object anyway! Moving permalloy! (*He crunches it up and throws it aside.*)

HALINA. Neville, just leave us for a moment, both of you, please, wait for me outside now.

WAVENEY (*very animated to* PEIRCE). You really are a fool as well as a shit, if you can't see she's worth having, worth keeping (*Loud.*) why don't you take me instead, if you have to have someone! Fair exchange! let me take the chair (*Loud.*) are you interested? . . .

HALINA. Waveney.

NEVILLE (*at exit*). Don't say anything further to him Halina.

WAVENEY. Give him nothing. (*Both exit leaving door open.*)

HALINA *sitting on wooden chair in lilac dress facing* PEIRCE.

HALINA. Now.

PEIRCE (*facing her*). Yes?

HALINA. How simple that must have seemed, you caught me off guard for one instant.

PEIRCE. That's all it needs.

HALINA (*getting up, picking up paper spike from his desk*). You got me to relax, let my defence slip, by talking about yourself. Not bad. (*Turning on him.*) I made one mistake which is not, I repeat *not*, going to prove fatal. I have no intention of letting it.

She swings round with a sharp but controlled movement and drives paper spike into wall, as her frustration boils.

You shouldn't keep these things on your desk, somebody next time might go between your eyes.

PEIRCE. I have had some near misses with those, yes.

He moves other spike carefully into a drawer. HALINA *facing him.*

HALINA. What do I have to do to get in?

PEIRCE. Do?

HALINA. How small do I have to make myself? What shape do I have to become to squeeze myself in, to crawl through the net?

What do you want me to say? What international incident needs to erupt to make me suddenly useful and desirable?

PEIRCE. I'm afraid it may not be possible now.

HALINA (*suddenly powerful*). Let me in! You have to. You're not certain about the decision, that's clear, I can feel it.

(*Straight at him:*) LET ME IN!

PEIRCE. Don't do that please. First time you've tried to bludgeon me with direct appeals, they never work, I can promise you.

HALINA (*looking at him*). They might (*Slight pause.*) I *have* to get in you know. (*With force:*) How many other people have you seen standing right here, trying for the same thing?

TURKISH WOMAN *outside in the passage, seen through the open door, calling in support in Turkish to her.*

At least somebody's on my side.

PEIRCE (*watching her*). Occasionally you know, I wonder if I changed places with a passenger what sort of place, and people would be staring at me as I came in to land.

HALINA (*straight back*). It won't work a second time! That technique.

Music in distance.

PEIRCE (*matter-of-fact*). I *really* do hate the idea of the party.

Moves.

It was good your story, very professional — rather, and this is a very uncharacteristic word for me . . . a wonderful lie.

HALINA (*very sharp*). *Who* says it's a lie?

PEIRCE. I do.

HALINA. You haven't proved that yet. And until you do, I think I have a chance.

PEIRCE. What would you have done in this country anyway if you'd managed it?

HALINA (*with feeling, looking about her*). I would have done just fine. (*Correcting herself:*) I will do.

PEIRCE (*facing her from behind the desk*). Sometimes, even quite often, I come across passengers I find personally appealing, people seething with energy, with things to offer — of more interest than most of the people who work in this building.

One finds oneself thinking why on earth shouldn't I recommend to let them in, that their application is valid.

HALINA. That's what you're going to do now.

PEIRCE. *NO.*

HALINA *sitting on chair, looking straight at him, they face each other.*

HALINA. You seem quite a reasonable man, though you need careful watching.

She leans forward.

Of all the thousands of people you've processed through this building, you can make *one* exception, (*Loud:*) who will ever know! The building won't fall down — not because of that anyway.

PEIRCE (*calmly*). I'd never be able to do this job again. This is the best controlled border in the Western World, the UK, and I'm the best in this building — though I wasn't at my best today.

That is the only thing that makes it worthwhile. (*Pause.*) Just.

Staring straight at her. Music playing.

I will do everything in my power to stop you getting into this country.

TURKISH WOMAN *calling at door.*

HALINA. You are *not* going to succeed though. I've lost the skirmish maybe, but I am still going to win (*Indicating* TURKISH WOMAN.) I am not going to look like that in a few days time.

PEIRCE. You have an appeal against our decision — but I must warn you, you'll find we can use the Media too.

HALINA. We'll see.

She stands very calm and strong in the middle of the stage, smoking.

Now my friend, I think we understand each other, you are going to tell me something of great interest.

She looks at him.

Who betrayed me?

PEIRCE. I can't tell you that.

HALINA. I think you can. I think you know and you quite want to tell me. *Who was it?*

Pause.

PEIRCE (*staring at her*). IF you ask me the right questions about that, Miss Rodziewizowna, I may be able to reply.

Blackout

Scene Five

A smear of Christmas carols, mixed with seasonal adverts, followed by the news, a news story about HALINA, 'the case of the mock execution housewife . . . Red Halina . . . Home Office spokesman, her story under investigation has proved a pack of lies . . . Future uncertain'. Sense of channels being switched, pieces of other stories about HALINA come piling on top of each other, a blitzkrieg of anti-stories 'lying Halina . . . KGB plant? . . . Polish housewife spreads fraudulent stories . . . attempt to undermine media credibility . . .'

ANDREW *and* NEVILLE *stand with back to audience frontstage, the walls of the office have slid back, the mural on the back wall is in shadows, bare stage with just two wooden floorboards leaning against wall and a roll of wallpaper.*

ANDREW. What on earth's happening here?

NEVILLE (*staring towards floorboards*). I had a compulsion to redecorate the flat — of course now they have ripped everything up, they are stopping for two weeks over Christmas! Leaving it looking like a war zone. I can't find where anything is.

Pause.

ANDREW. Have you seen her?

NEVILLE. Of course not. Have you?

Loud crash, another floorboard is thrown on stage. Both ANDREW *and* NEVILLE *start.*

ANDREW. No. Have you seen this? The evening paper? (*He waves it.*) 'Red Halina, mad housewife, KGB prankster, a weaver of falsehoods, malicious intent etc. . .'

They are making out she was sent by the Russians to be deliberately rumbled, so as to discredit any future unfavourable reports coming out of the Eastern Block! (*Flicks paper.*) There's even a cartoon.

NEVILLE. I have to admit I've rather enjoyed some of the things that have been said about her!

ANDREW (*sharp*). Really?

NEVILLE. And she may well have had quite an irresponsible effect.

ANDREW (*sharp*). She didn't intend to! (*Pause.*) Somebody informed on her.

NEVILLE. I had a dream about her the other night. (*Slight smile.*) very easy to interpret like most of my dreams. Halina as this small curly-haired girl staring at me through a wire fence, asking me for a cigarette, then this mad bloated old tramp,

covered all over in travel labels, outside the window, refusing
to look at me. Like some batty avenging angel clawing her way
out of obscurity, up the side of the house, but refusing to
meet my eyes.

He moves.

They've moved so quickly! I never expected it, detaining her,
locking her up, the deportation order. I wasn't even here when
they took her away!

ANDREW. They're like large reptiles, departments in the Home
Office, most of the time they don't move at all, lying
motionless in the sun, but when they want to, they can move
like hell.

Another crash, a second floorboard thrown across the stage.

NEVILLE (*looking at* ANDREW's *pale face*). You look terrible.

ANDREW. Thank you. I feel it too.

NEVILLE. Why?

ANDREW. The contrasts in my life are particularly clear at this
time of year. I went to a party last night, when I got there I
realised it was a theme party, fancy dress, do you know what
it was, a *fin de siècle* party!

NEVILLE. My God already!

ANDREW. Yes, everything and everybody dressed in black and
white, people into end of the century ennui into celebrating
their boredom, the years are silting up for them already.

NEVILLE. Silting, that's right, people with no appetite for
anything . . .

ANDREW. Imagine London in the nineties, if it's like this now!

And then I raced off to one of my absurd rendezvous, in a
deserted bus station at one o'clock in the morning, with a
Cypriot family. The people I *manage* to get in usually have a
pretty miserable time. It's such a waste. Some of them
disappear without trace. They think they are coming to a land
of opportunity, a multi-racial society! A home! (*Very sharp.*)
God knows if I've ever actually helped anybody!

NEVILLE. Of course you have.

ANDREW (*suddenly turning on him*). You think so do you — that's your considered opinion is it Neville?

NEVILLE *startled by his tone.*

I know you've always found what I've done pretty ridiculous, really rather comic.

NEVILLE (*very surprised*). I have!

ANDREW. Yes, of course you have. So I. don't really need your reassurance now.

NEVILLE. What's the matter Andrew?

ANDREW. Time for me to scuttle off to another meeting.

NEVILLE. But what will happen to Halina?

ANDREW. What indeed? She's dangling on the edge. Her future doesn't look too bright does it?

ANDREW *moving.*

NEVILLE. Why on earth wouldn't she accept the original plan Andrew?

Pause.

ANDREW. You don't understand that? That's easy.

He looks straight at NEVILLE.

Who would want to land right *here* — if they could possibly help it?

Blackout.

A still of a rather fetching small girl in forties clothes appears on the screen, she is staring gravely at us through a fence.

Scene Six

The sound of aircraft taking off and landing very loud. A metal grid slides across the whole length of the mural on the back wall, the mural visible through the metal mesh.

A door with a barred grid upstage, left of the back wall.

The world at the detention centre, on the edge of the runway, among the warehouses at the airport. Carols grinding out, only half audibly from a tannoy, foreign voices calling, visitors' area, a wooden table and two chairs, upstage a second table and chairs.

HALINA is standing, she is wearing a plain black dress, and looks elegant. She has a bruise around her eye. WAVENEY is standing holding a large bag.

WAVENEY (*as planes go directly overhead*). Christ! The planes fly so low here they are scraping the top of the building! Is it always like this?

HALINA. Yes, you feel all you have to do is stretch out and you could easily grab hold of a passing under-carriage and get a flight out of here.

WAVENEY (*calling up as one goes over*). Clapped out old planes. Really have to heave themselves into the air, probably start falling out of the sky. (*She moves.*) It's a weird place to put a prison, right at the end of a runway. (*She points to brightly-coloured saris drying on the radiators.*) Clothes from all over the world drying here. Look . . . (*She delves into her bag.*) I brought you a Christmas present.

HALINA. You shouldn't have.

WAVENEY. Somewhere in here. (*Bits of plastic fly out of bag.*) I ground up a fistful of styluses, (*To* HALINA:) styli, pulverised the moving permalloy, (*Scatters fragments.*) all that remains of them and the shop, ashes of a sun-rise store!

HALINA. Good.

WAVENEY (*produces present*). I brought you an atlas.

HALINA. An atlas? So I can improve my Polish geography!

WAVENEY. No. So you can select where you're going to go. Stick a finger in the world.

HALINA (*smiles*). There's no point — nobody will have me. I've been refused permission everywhere.

WAVENEY. Really? There must be somewhere on the whole planet — what about the Falkland Islands!

HALINA (*slight smile*).You have to draw the line somewhere. (*She moves.*)

Anyway it's been *here* that I wanted to come to, not America or Paris but here. Always — Now I can't get into any country, I'm being sent back to Poland.

WAVENEY. What's going to happen to you there?

HALINA. God knows.

WAVENEY. I'm sorry. (*She moves.*) You know I told that bastard immigration officer to take me instead — I don't think that's such a bad idea? (*Sharp smile.*) I mean I haven't exactly got much to keep me here. If I could take my little girl, and if there was anywhere to go, which there isn't! (*Shouts at back wall.*) So don't get any ideas! (*Ironic smile.*) Do you think anybody would notice the difference if I changed places with you, (*She laughs.*) I don't think so, if I just wear your hat and did your walk.

HALINA. You are certainly welcome to the Christmas dinner I'm going to get here.

Plane going over.

WAVENEY. What a strangled wail that one's got!

I know I hitched a ride on what you were doing, your campaign, for no real reason. I projected your story so big on such a large screen maybe it seemed more important, more likely to win, than it really was.

HALINA. Don't be stupid, it's not your fault. (*She turns.*) I've been so obsessed with getting in, I haven't thought about you Waveney, and you losing your job.

WAVENEY. Yes. I don't much like this feeling I can tell you — hard as I try it's like I always return to the same place. I used to think I was just waiting till my luck changed, I don't now.

It's very simple, why shouldn't I do something with my life for chrissake.

Voices calling from building with anger.

And I don't like what's happening inside me either.

(*She turns.*) Anyway — a real Christmas present would be me finding a way of springing you from here in the next 24 hours wouldn't it?

NEVILLE *enters in grey suit carrying briefcase.*

NEVILLE. Halina — there you are. (*He looks around him.*) For some reason I thought the bars would be a little more discreet.

HALINA (*staring at him across the stage*). You always look so crisp Neville.

WAVENEY. He certainly looks like a lawyer doesn't he.

NEVILLE. What has happened to your face Halina?

HALINA. It's a bruise.

NEVILLE. I can see that.

HALINA *is half turned away.*

HALINA (*lightly*). It's shaped like a strawberry don't you think?

NEVILLE (*sharp*). You are not going to tell me you were beaten up by maniacal guards — they strapped you to the floor I suppose.

HALINA (*firmly*). No. I did it myself. I suddenly lost control, I wanted to get out of here rather a lot.

NEVILLE. And you did that?

WAVENEY. Yes.

NEVILLE (*to* WAVENEY). Now — I have some business to conduct. (*Moving.*) I have come to help Halina. Only one visitor is allowed in here with you at a time, and to make sure we're left alone — (*He looks at her.*) I will tell you who informed on you to the Immigration authorities.

WAVENEY. You know who betrayed her?

HALINA *with her back to him, not moving.*

HALINA. Tell me, I'm interested.

Pause.

NEVILLE. It was I. (*She doesn't move.*) *Me.* I did it.

WAVENEY. My God. *YOU* — why didn't I think of that? It fits doesn't it.

HALINA (*turning from wall, loud*). Leave me alone with him!

(*Quieter.*) Please. You can come back a little later to check if he's still alive.

WAVENEY. Yes. (*Sharp smile.*) I'll try not to get locked up back there as one of the inmates. (*In exit.*) Be careful Halina, never take your eyes off him.

WAVENEY *exits.*

NEVILLE. I informed on you. I supplied the necessary information on you.

HALINA. You lousy . . . fucking bastard.

NEVILLE (*facing her*). That's what I did, Halina, yes.

Pause.

HALINA. But *in fact* you see, you didn't.

NEVILLE. What on earth do you mean?

HALINA. It wasn't you at all. You had nothing to do with it.

The person who informed on me was one of my fellow Poles — one of our group.

(*Staring across at him*). If you did try to do it . . .

NEVILLE (*loud*). I did do it! I did!

HALINA. You couldn't it seems even do that properly. It was obviously unrecorded.

NEVILLE (*swings round, very sharp*). God — does absolutely *NOTHING* work in this country (*Loud.*) can't even rely on their informing service!

He stops and looks at her.

My one big action . . . my spontaneous and dark manoeuvre, and nobody gets to hear about it.

HALINA. Precisely.

Sound of people, voices, foreign calls and shouts from the bowels of the building, increasing in volume.

NEVILLE. Don't you want to know why I did it?

HALINA. No. I know why you did it.

NEVILLE. No you don't, you don't at all. I did it because I knew you were heading straight for disaster. I had to make you see sense, before it was too late.

HALINA (*straight at him*). Really?

NEVILLE (*watching her*). Why should I believe you anyway, you are probably lying like you usually are.

I can't trust you about anything.

HALINA (*loud*). You not trust *me!*

NEVILLE. No. (*moving around.*) Why do I keep getting the feeling that all of this was planned?

HALINA. What was planned?

NEVILLE. My world being deliberately turned upside down, a carefully structured and malevolent scheme — leading to my outrageous humiliation at the hands of the immigration officer. Fortunately I've discovered my job is safe — I think. (*Loud.*) I had to justify my existence to him — me — in my own city!

HALINA. That was due to your incompetence and clumsiness.

NEVILLE. It was pure malice.

HALINA. And you think I had something to do with that!

NEVILLE (*shrewd look*). I don't know. It's very strange isn't it, we had a straightforward plan, which you decided to reject.

HALINA. Yes.

NEVILLE. And what have you managed instead, what have you actually achieved? One tiny and brief piece of fame, ending in you being torn apart, and a jousting match with an immigration officer for an afternoon.

HALINA. One of the best afternoons of my life.

NEVILLE. Before he cracked you and you lost everything. That's *all* your extraordinary decision has —

HALINA (*advancing on him with aggression and precision*). The really interesting question is not about me at all. It's about *you*. Why a fairly successful solicitor should want to enter into this scheme in the first place — and I'll tell you the answer.

NEVILLE. I rather felt you might.

HALINA. Because you thought you were in need of a little distraction, isn't that right, to get rid of the stale claustrophobia you were in, all around you, bored with life, here was a nice idea for a little suspense. And the candidate was this weird spiky Polish woman — might provide a few comfortable surprises.

NEVILLE. I'm absolutely sick of being told what I'm feeling by you, that I'm predictable, have no imagination.

HALINA (*advancing on him*). And I knew this desire of yours, this *mild* need could vanish overnight, before the marriage, cancellation, leaving me nowhere at all. Or worse, far, far worse, it could continue *after* the arrangement was over, this new interest of yours, and you'd return again and again to have a look, you'd have a claim on me, I'd be one of your possessions.

NEVILLE. My God you're so pleased with yourself Halina! The thought never crossed my mind.

HALINA (*moving*). Especially when you started being intrigued by this tiny pimple of history; having her right there.

NEVILLE. *I* never called you that, I did not . . .

HALINA. And when my real history, the slow drip drip of my existence with my father was far too humdrum to get me in, and I had to expand myself, give myself a little notoriety that proved even better, didn't it —

NEVILLE. That's not true.

HALINA (*loud*). And when you saw this appetite for nearly everything coming out of me, this hunger, straightforward selfish hunger, spurting everywhere, all over your apartment, and over other parts of your life, that was even *more* interesting (*Straight at him.*) almost fascinating.

Staring at him.

So you decided to own me after all didn't you. (*Straight at him.*) Simple!

She moves.

And now I'm locked up here with all these other caged people, feeling like me, beating on the walls, you should hear all the different languages echoing around here! And I can't do anything about it. I can't get myself out in time. (*Loud with anger.*) I'm not enjoying it. I hate myself for losing.

Silence.

NEVILLE (*drily*). Marry me.

HALINA *by wall not facing him.*

HALINA. For what reason?

NEVILLE. Don't start that Halina — you know the reason.

Faces appearing at the grid staring in at them, noises and echoes from the rest of building.

NEVILLE. Because you're in a brutally simple situation. You took on enormous odds and lost. If you're thrown out of this country, which you're going to be in 48 hours time, you're finished. You won't have done anything with your life and you never will.

Slight pause.

HALINA. That's not good enough Neville.

NEVILLE (*very sharp*). What do you mean it's not good enough? (*Moving.*) And *I* don't want to see your life a total waste Halina, I certainly don't want you on my conscience.

HALINA. What's the other reason?

Faces at the grid watching them.

NEVILLE (*furious*). I'm not going to be interrogated by you, treated like this, as if I'm

HALINA (*cutting him off, not facing him*). Why else Neville?

Pause. A plane taking off nearby.

NEVILLE (*not looking at her*). All right — Because over the last few weeks I've been propelled out of my normal existence. (*Moving, not looking at her.*) You know people that almost die, like in a car crash, for a moment they actually stop breathing and find themselves floating out of themselves and staring down from above at their own bodies, and surroundings — for once I forget the medical term for it — I've had that without the crash, find myself peering at a world full of dying video shops, with graveyards for their machines, black girls full of startling hostility towards me from the first moment they see me! Those disturbed carol singers, outside the window, and old clients pursuing me full of dark city paranoia — even immigration officers that read Dostoevsky! It's like a map of the city where all the streets have been re-named.

Slight pause.

(*Sharp*). I've been evicted from my normal certainty Halina, and the person responsible for that is you.

HALINA (*not facing him*). Quite possibly, yes.

NEVILLE. While lying through your teeth about everything else — you've revealed things to me! Whether deliberately or not, I still don't know; You've never said anything about what you feel about being here, about how you find this country.

HALINA. I told you I wouldn't till I'd lived here — so you'll be spared that now.

NEVILLE (*very sharp*). What right you had to cause all this, I have no idea, but you have.

Pause.

Will that do? (*Sharp.*) So marry me.

Plane taking off.

Halina, don't try to be so calm, we're here in this ghastly

place, with all these trapped people.

Indicating faces clamouring at the grid.

You can't get out of it any other way.

HALINA. You reckon that is so do you?

NEVILLE (*sharp*). I think you have a duty to stay here now.

HALINA *turns.*

HALINA. A duty! (*Forced laugh.*) 'England needs me' you mean . . . I don't think so! (*She moves.*) And tell me — how would you categorise our relationship, Neville.

NEVILLE (*loud*). Don't do this.

HALINA (*loud*). How?

NEVILLE (*loud*). You really infuriate me, Halina!

Pause staring at her.

It's hardly *love* that's for certain.

HALINA. Love? No.

NEVILLE. God knows if we'll ever touch each other either.

HALINA (*with full agreement*). Yes.

NEVILLE. I . . . I don't know why you're doing this . . .

Slight pause, watching her.

I suppose if I have to describe it, if you're making me, I suppose I'm impaled on you. (*Watching her.*) On this Polish spike.

HALINA. That's better.

NEVILLE (*loud*). Don't patronise me, Halina.

HALINA *moves.*

HALINA. Yes — snarled together.

NEVILLE (*louder*). Snarled, *yes.* (*Looking across at her.*) What are your feelings for me?

HALINA. I like you (*Pause.*) quite.

NEVILLE (*loud*). No quites — you're not allowed any *quites.* None.

Noises of bells, end of visting hours.

HALINA. Time for you to go.

NEVILLE (*furious, passionate with anger*). For chrissake,
Halina — don't be so incredibly proud and obstinate. You're
too proud to do this, aren't you!

He hurls chair against wall.

HALINA. There're people watching Neville please.

Couple of the faces applauding from behind grid.

NEVILLE (*really angry*). I don't care who's, watching — you
want to be like them, stay amongst them do you, wherever
they're going, be locked up for the rest of your life! (*Shouts.*)
You stupid, perverse woman. You need to do it!

HALINA. Neville . . .

NEVILLE *grabs her and gives her a violent shake.*

NEVILLE. Don't you realise, you need me, you've got to accept
that, you need to do this, you do!

HALINA. I need you . . .?

NEVILLE (*loud*). Yes! Halina — see some sense now.

People at the grid.

Are you going to do it or not?

*Plane suddenly flies directly over them, much lower than all
the rest. As it does so* HALINA *replies.*

HALINA. I need you . . . maybe . . .

NEVILLE. What did you say?

HALINA. You mean you weren't listening.

Noise and bells, plane dying away in distance.

I don't want to. But I said maybe.

NEVILLE. Maybe!

Noise of plane dying away.

HALINA. Will they let us get married?

NEVILLE. If we make them believe it. IF we're seen a lot

together. And if we live in the same place afterwards for say a six-month period.

HALINA *turns.*

HALINA. Three months.

NEVILLE. Four months.

HALINA *nods.*

Do you want a contract to that effect, that it won't be longer.

HALINA. No. . . . (*Slight pause.*) Not yet.

Sound of doors being locked, slamming shut.

You're probably locked in now for Christmas.

NEVILLE. Good, my apartment is a wreck because of you, the oil went everywhere. At least I can keep an eye on you.

HALINA. You mean we're glued that tight together — already? When you move, I move. I'm not sure I like the idea of that at all.

NEVILLE (*sharply*). It's happened.

HALINA (*sound of aircraft in distance, she moves to grid*). What a place to get engaged, among the warehouses, and this low flat prison, and the cages full of quarantining animals, both monkeys and people locked up around here, and the dead planes parked amongst the long grass, and all the other flotsam of the airport. I've been pushed right into the jaws of the exit.

NEVILLE. You've dragged me with you there, too. One of the edges of the country, you can look back into it from here. Have you noticed, the snow's gone at last Halina, the mild weather's returned. (*Looks at her.*) At least now I may have put a stop to the careering nightmare you've put me through.

Pause.

Of course this might mean merely a continuation. . . .

HALINA (*moving*). Yes.

She stares back at him.

Or even just the start.

Blackout.